I0818493

ROBERT LONGO

ROBERT LONGO

HIRMER

Edited by
Elsy Lahner and Klaus Albrecht Schröder

ALBERTINA

CONTENTS

FOREWORD

Klaus Albrecht Schröder

It has been a good twenty years since we were able to reopen the Albertina Museum in 2003 with Robert Longo's exhibition of *The Freud Drawings*. In my last year as Director General of the Albertina Museum, we can now look back at these beginnings and dedicate a comprehensive exhibition to this outstanding American artist.

The show features important key works from the various periods of his production, beginning with *Men in the Cities*, the series that made him famous overnight and embodied the zeitgeist of early 1980s New York like few other works. The exhibition also presents the *Bodyhammers*, in which the artist expresses his unease with gun culture in the United States, as well as works from the Freud cycle. The latter is based on photographs secretly taken in Freud's office and apartment for documentation purposes, before he had to flee from the Nazis to London in 1938. Also featured are works from *God Machines*, in which Longo addresses monotheistic world religions, and *The Destroyer Cycle*, in which he takes up events from global politics.

Robert Longo is known for his monumental hyperrealistic works: powerful, dynamic charcoal drawings whose virtuoso technique and the visual force of the motifs mesmerize the observer. For his models, Longo uses photographs that record dramatic situations at the moment of their greatest tension. The artist is concerned here with the depiction of power—in nature, politics, history. He utilizes visual material that has been reproduced thousands of times, and which has long been a part of pop culture, of our collective visual memory. Longo isolates and reduces the motifs so as to raise their visual impact to a higher power. By enlarging the subject and intensifying the lighting into a dramatic chiaroscuro, we find ourselves before gigantic, previously unseen theatrical images. Longo draws on existing images, references reality secondhand, and creates impressive "copies" of the original black-and-white photographs, which pale beside their transformation into colossal charcoal drawings.

The dramatic lighting and shadow effects of the charcoal drawings emphasize the objects' plasticity and the spatial depth. They make the motif appear as real as it is unreal. The deep black of the charcoal rubbed into the paper swallows up all of the light. Paradoxically, Longo is ultimately capable, like no one else, of evoking brightness and radiant light, transparency, and differentiated materiality with the blackness of charcoal.

It is my great pleasure to be able to present this unique exhibition during my last year at the Albertina Museum. The show will travel in a modified form to the Louisiana Museum of Modern Art in Humlebæk, Denmark, in April 2025.

A project like this depends on the participation of many. For this reason, I would like to express my profound gratitude to all those who have contributed to its realization. First and foremost, my heartfelt thanks go to the artist. This exhibition would never have been possible without the intensive support of Robert Longo and his team. I likewise wholeheartedly thank the lenders for their willingness to lend us their artworks for the duration of the exhibition, and for the confidence they have shown in our museum. My immeasurable gratitude goes in particular to Siegfried and Jutta Weishaupt, the main and most important collectors of Robert Longo's work. Without the significant loans from the breathtaking collection of these major collectors, the exhibition would not have attained such scope, profundity, and quality. I also thank all those who, through generous gifts, have contributed to the artist being represented in our own collection with important works, in particular Otto and Christa Schwarz, who early on acquired a fine collection of preliminary studies for Robert Longo's monumental works and ultimately donated them to the Albertina Museum—today precious jewels of our collection. Special thanks go to the Thaddaeus Ropac Gallery and the Pace Gallery for their valuable support and extremely good cooperation.

The curator of this extensive project, Elsy Lahner, and assistant curator, Melissa Lumbroso, both deserve my special gratitude. As do Christiane Steinbichler-Schranz for the exhibition management, Sandra Maria Rust for the catalogue management, and Christian Schienerl for the graphic design of the publication. In addition, I thank the team at Hirmer Publishing, along with the translators and copy editors for the pleasant and productive collaboration. Last but not least, my thanks go to the authors: Cindy Sherman for her accompanying words, and Holger Liebs and Isabelle Graw, whose essay and interview with the artist provide us with excellent insights into the work of Robert Longo and underscore the importance of this extraordinary artist.

p. 6
Installation view, The Albertina Museum, Vienna
The Freud Drawings, 2003
Photo: Margherita Spiluttini (detail)

p. 9
Installation view, The Albertina Museum, Vienna
Schwarz Weiß & Grau, 2020/21

pp. 10/11, 12/13
Installation view, Deichtorhallen, Hamburg
Proof: Francisco Goya, Sergei Eisenstein, Robert Longo
2018

PROF. Dr. FREUD
3-4

RECORDS OF OUR TIMES

Elsy Lahner

*As an artist, I feel a moral imperative to preserve
the images of our shared dystopic present
with the hope that something will one day change.*[1]

◀ **FIG. 1** Robert Longo
Untitled (Bullet Hole, Earth Day, 2017, UA in Huntsville), 2018
detail from pp. 102/103

▸ **FIG. 2** Installation view, Metro Pictures, New York, *Magellan*, 1997/98

It is one of Robert Longo's most impressive and at the same time most poignant works: *Untitled (Raft at Sea)* (2016–17; PP. 12, 184/185) depicts a rubber dinghy on the high seas, overloaded with its cargo of refugees and dangerously low in the water. The people sitting on the edge of the rubber ring, mostly men, are disturbingly close to the water's surface. They wear caps, hats, and thick jackets under their life vests, indicating the inhospitable temperatures. The composition situates the boat on the horizon line in the upper third of the image, on the central panel of the monumental charcoal drawing. The entire area underneath is the dark sea with its turbulent waves, to which the dinghy and its passengers are exposed. An overcast sky stretches above, becoming less clouded over to the right—at least promising a little hope. We observe the scene not from a secure perspective from above, from a larger ship, or from the air, but on the same level as the rubber raft. We might, therefore, be in a similar dinghy or even in the water amid the waves. The artist has thus placed us in the same predicament as the people shown in his drawing, who are risking their lives to flee.

For *Raft at Sea*, Longo draws on an image we have often seen in the media in recent years. Yet in the whirlwind of images that swirl around us every day, we no longer perceive the situation in all of its harrowing intensity, because we have, to a certain degree, become accustomed to it. Through the artist's altered composition and the enormous size of the work, Longo forces us to look once more and to engage with what is presented.

Rendering this image as a drawing is essential as the transformation of the original visual material into another medium triggers an altered mode of attention. The theatrical black and white of the charcoal drawing, especially the lighting effects and chiaroscuro, transmit in hyperrealistic overemphasis the dramatic atmosphere that the portrayed situation requires. Through the process of drawing, Longo slows down the speed at which images rush at us. In doing so, the drawing functions as a deacceleration, a pause.

In the late 1970s Longo belonged to the so-called Pictures Generation, a loose grouping of New York artists that critically engaged with mass media and pop culture in their works. His iconic large-scale series of drawings *Men in the Cities* (1979–83; PP. 31-39) in their extreme, dynamic poses aptly expressed the fragile mood— fraught with tension— of the 1980s. New York in those days was dominated as much by financial wealth, a real estate boom, and yuppie culture as it was by rising criminality, drug problems, and social inequality, polarizing the city. The neoconservative politics of the Reagan era and the threat posed by the Cold War contributed to a climate of insecurity. Longo's severely formal drawings echo this sentiment. The figures are dressed in "urban uniforms and Film Noir attire"[2] against a white background, in an empty space, each one isolated, frozen in a moment of intense movement and physical contortion. The artist found a correspondence in the intensely stylized representation of black-and-white contrasts, originating in news media and black-and-white films.[3] Longo prefers these abstract symbols to be installed as a group in order to create a rhythmic tension. He thereby also articulates their individually experienced inner turmoil in a collectively lived structure marked by tension and pressure.

After *Men in the Cities*, Longo shifted his artistic practice in various directions. He created his *Combines* series (1981–89), montages that fused different images and media in a single work. He made sculptures and worked

on film projects. The foundations for his current artistic practice, however, were laid out about a decade later. He describes how, after the conclusion of his elaborate cyber-punk thriller *Johnny Mnemonic* (1995), when he once again had more time to spend at home, he observed his young sons watching television.[4] It made him aware of how numb he himself had become to the media: "All these images that exist on a daily basis, that enter you, quietly, seamlessly. And you have no idea what's happening to you."[5]

This inspired him to make a drawing every single day for a year. Each day, he selected an image to document the present, which he felt needed to be recorded and could not be allowed to simply disappear. It could be something that leaped to his eye or that he deliberately searched for: the image of a child or an athlete, a photograph from the newspaper, scenes on the street such as a police raid or a dead body on the sidewalk, an advertisement, or a film still. *Magellan* (1996; FIG. 2), created in this manner, encompasses 366 smaller drawings[6] and includes many of the motifs from Longo's subsequent visual repertoire and can therefore serve as a lexicon for everything that followed. With this series, Longo developed his approach towards understanding images and learning to read them, to literally record them and thus to bear witness.

While the *Magellan* drawings were executed on vellum with black marker, graphite, and charcoal, Longo arrived at his present-day technique shortly afterwards. The photograph of a gigantic wave in a surfing magazine inspired him to convert it into a large format drawing. Since all he had in his studio at the time were charcoal sticks—which he actually hated and considered incredibly imprecise—Longo began to draw with them out of necessity, which accelerated the drawing process. Not only could parts be covered with color faster and more brutally without long drying times—compared with painting—the charcoal was also easier to rework and manipulate. Having graduated with a degree in sculpture, Longo learned to appreciate the sculptural method, when the drawing could be worked over with the eraser as though with a chisel, blurring it with the finger, and rubbing the charcoal into the paper (FIG. 3). It fascinated him that he could create highly aggressive images with the aid of a light material, with coal dust. The works themselves were marked, moreover, by a powerful symbolism of death, given that charcoal is made from burned deadwood.

Longo's drawings, which he regards as pictures in the tradition of painting, are created layer by layer in the most varied nuances of color between 50 percent black, halftone black, normal black, or black black, warm or cold black.[7] He sometimes employs charcoal sticks and sometimes applies the dust of ground charcoal with a brush, exposing the white underneath it later on. In contrast to traditional painting, in which the image is built up from dark to light, with white lighting accents added towards the end, Longo works from light to dark. He begins with the white of the paper, which, as such, remains untreated, concentrates on the various shades of gray, and does add the darkest and deepest black at the end.

However, Longo is never primarily interested in the technical perfection of his drawings: "I have never been into the virtuosity of technique."[8] As a conceptual artist, he is much more concerned with expression, meaning, and the emotional impact of his works. For him, it is vital to reproduce images as quickly as possible, yet by hand, so as to be able to capture them. He realized early on that he needed the help of a team in his studio to produce such works.[9] Longo develops the idea and concept of his works, selects the sources of the images, the basis for his works, experiments with these in detailed studies in a small format, and fine tunes them. His assistants then take over tasks such as transferring the basic drawing to a larger format or executing the time-consuming rendering, sometimes taking a full year to make.

In order to generate the best possible version of an image, the visual source is modified, for example by depicting a shark's teeth much larger than in the original. The image is often constructed from parts of different images, so that the tiger we see in the drawing does not correspond to a single photograph, but rather to Longo's ideal image of a tiger (P. 93). Fragments of the first waves (PP. 72/73) on which the artist worked on derive from images of the smoke from the collapsing towers of the World Trade Center. Longo replaced the reflections of the camera in the visors of the fighter jet pilots' helmets (P. 83) with views of the sky that the pilots could see. The reflections in the black door of Sigmund Freud's apartment were emphasized in order to recall the lighting spectacle at the Nuremberg Nazi Party rallies.

The dramatics and the composition of an image play a central role in Longo's work. For *God Machines* (2008–11; PP. 109–115), his portrayal of places of worship, he creates an atmosphere of reverence and sublimity through overwhelming size, through light and shadow, as well as through the perspective that expresses the power of religious institutions. A detailed elaboration of a bullet hole in close-up (FIG. 1), which allows the observer to recognize every crack and every splitter in the glass, literally draws us into the

▶ **FIG. 3** Close-up of a charcoal drawing by Robert Longo

violence of the moment. By precisely rendering the mushroom cloud **(P. 87)** in central perspective, the artist transmits not only the enormous power, brutality, and destructive force of the catastrophic event of an atom bomb exploding, but also the feeling of fascination in the face of the terrifying beauty of this phenomenon.

Raised in the age of American film epics such as *The Ten Commandments* (1956), *Ben Hur* (1959), and *Spartacus* (1960), Longo strives to create works that mesmerize the public through their dramatic staging and emotional intensity: "I wanted to make epic art."[10] In his charcoal drawings, he appropriates the pathos, aesthetics, and narrative of film, the visual language of the cinema. Drawing on his experience as a film director and his work on music videos for bands such as New Order and R.E.M., Longo often brings a cinematic gaze to the creation of his works. His motifs recall film stills that capture a moment of tension, an emotional climax. This dramatic component is experienced anew every time we see a work, as if it is happening right now, thereby acquiring a timeless quality.

Longo chooses motifs whose essence are symbols for freedom, power, and passion: the huge breaking wave **(PP. 96-97)**, the shark with its jaws wide open **(PP. 94-95)**, or a lushly blooming rose **(P. 161)**. By employing certain symbols, figures, or themes, he represents in his works archetypes that embody the fundamental experiences and emotions found in the history of humankind. *Raft at Sea*, for example, picks up on a current topic by depicting the present situation of refugees, while also making an obvious reference to Théodore Géricault's painting *The Raft of the Medusa* (1818–19). In this manner, Longo demonstrates that history repeats itself. Similar to Géricault's work, which addresses the struggle for survival of the socially disadvantaged on the raft, *Raft at Sea* also contains social criticism. It illuminates the experiences of hardship, despair, and hope, along with the fight against the forces of nature. Above all, it points to the harsh reality of social inequality and the moral background to political decisions.

Longo's visual universe is fueled by personal impressions, influences, and topics connected with U.S. society, politics, and pop culture, as well as significant global events. Police brutality and racism, war and terrorism, the exercise of power, repression, and violence all find expression in his works. Yet even if the motifs appear personal, the artist is not concerned alone with the expression of an individual emotion. *Untitled (Daddy's Caddy)* (2010; **PP. 100/101**) is an example of this. The title refers to the car that belonged to Longo's father, who never bought a new car, purchasing instead the used cars of his boss. Aside from the biographical aspect, the Cadillac here—the front part of which disappears in the dark—represents a status symbol in the mentality of postwar United States. It embodies the American dream of success and social advancement and stands for innovation and modern technology, and with "fins like a Sci-fi rocket ship, it is as if it is plunging into darkness like the hero's journey to hell in a Greek Epic Poem."[11] On the other hand, the artist always tries to establish a personal

▸ **FIG. 4** Robert Longo's studio, New York City, with *Untitled (Iceberg For C.D.F.)*, 2016

connection to each of his images. For this reason, every drawing is preceded by a certain amount of research, in order to delve as far as possible into the topic. His objective is to achieve a balance between the socially relevant and the most personal meaning.

Longo sees himself as an abstract artist, who nevertheless works in a representational mode—similar to the way he previously rendered *Men in the Cities* as images, which he understood as signs. With this approach, he dealt intensively with the works of the Abstract Expressionists in a series of his own, examining not only their significance for American art, but also their influence on his own work.

Despite the hyperrealistic execution, abstract elements can, on closer examination, also be found in other drawings, such as when the black of the charcoal turns into a diffuse, indeterminable surface. His motifs, too, hover from time to time across the boundary between abstraction and figuration: in the tiger's pattern of stripes, in snow-covered trees, in the bricks of the Western Wall, or in the bullet holes in a pane of glass. The camouflage pattern of the net stretched over a group of Syrian and Iraqi refugees (PP. 175-177) to provide them with shade transforms the people in their individual clothing into a uniform mass. Longo operates in an intermediate zone, such that when viewing tank tire tracks in the snow, the first impression is in fact that of looking at an abstract work of art (PP. 178/179). Just as this work is based on a photograph taken by a drone, so the image of prisoners in Kandahar (PP. 152-155) was taken by an infrared camera from a great distance. His drawing reproduces the grain of the camera as well as the dot matrix of the newspaper in which the image was first published.

Untitled (Iceberg for C.D.F.) (2015–16; FIG. 4, PP. 128/129) also has abstract features, which are emphasized above all through the chosen image sections. The composition exposes very little of the sea on which the iceberg floats or of its other surroundings. Remarkably, this work is also a charcoal drawing, in which black is visible only in traces. Like Caspar David Friedrich, whom he references in the title, Longo uses the landscape as a backdrop to reflect on emotional states and on human existence in relationship to nature. The parallel lines and graduations in the lower part of the image result from the iceberg slowly melting, causing it to rise out of the water. Longo gives the majestic mountain the form of a crown, raising the question of whether humans can truly be considered the crown of creation or whether in fact it is nature itself. For despite the many political problems we are confronted with around the globe, climate change remains the most urgent existential challenge that we must face.

1 Robert Longo in conversation with the author on June 27, 2024.
2 The information and the following quotations are from a conversation between the artist and the author on February 22, 2024.
3 In addition to film and television, Longo was also influenced by the energy of the downtown punk and No Wave music scene. See the essay by Holger Liebs in this publication: Jerking into Now. Robert Longo's *Men in the Cities* and the Pictures Generation, 23–28.
4 See note 2.
5 See note 2.
6 There are 366 drawings because 1996 was a leap year.
7 https://www.theartistprofilearchive.com/artist-profiles/robert-longo/#video, Robert Longo in conversation with Sophie Chahinian, December 2017 [accessed June 27, 2024].
8 See note 2.
9 Just as many artworks by the Old Masters were created in cooperative workshops.
10 See note 2.
11 See note 2.

JERKING INTO NOW. ROBERT LONGO'S *MEN IN THE CITIES* AND THE PICTURES GENERATION

Holger Liebs

FIG. 1 Robert Longo, photographic studies for *Men in the Cities*, 1979

It is not by chance that they are sometimes confused: dance and the kind of movement you make when you are suddenly thrown off balance, whether by a shove, a jostle, or an even more violent impact. In both cases, similar groups of body muscles activate. In addition to the gluteus maximus of the hip joint and the quadriceps of the upper thigh, it is primarily the musculature of the trunk and the muscles of the calves and feet that are tensed. Differences exist, of course—especially in the degree of gracefulness—between the spontaneous contraction of muscles or spasmodic twitching as a reaction to the impact of massive external forces, and the purposeful and focused efforts to bend the body into the most elegant form possible in a gymnastic or athletic manner. In the former case, the limbs are involuntarily subjugated to external impulses, and in the latter case are arbitrarily controlled by internal ones. Strangely enough, however, there are times when both physical activities resemble one another.

But are there types of movements, dance styles, poses that are typical for a certain epoch or generation and later identified with it? In 1979, when Robert Longo began throwing objects, such as rubber balls, at friends dressed in business suits or skirt suits on the roof of his studio in South Street, in Manhattan's financial district, where he lived with Cindy Sherman, he was concerned with realizing an idea that had long been on his mind. Longo photographed how they bent, twisted, stretched, or fell as though they had just been pierced by a bullet, trying to capture a moment of movement that fluctuated between dancing, tumbling, being struck by a bullet, flying, falling, floating, or dying.

These photographs, in color or black and white, depict not only the members of Longo's peer group twisting to a predetermined—and yet quasi spontaneous—choreography, they also show in the background the skyscrapers of southern Manhattan, a three-masted ship anchored in the water, or the nearby Brooklyn Bridge (FIG. 1). These images were later published by Longo as an independent series.[1] Projected on the studio wall, they served as the templates for black charcoal drawings, in which the figures, positioned in front of a neutral white background, were isolated from their environment and removed from the spatial-temporal context of their creation. The resulting series, *Men in the Cities* (1979–83; PP. 31-39), became not only a crucial fixpoint in the history of American postwar art, but also free-floating pop-cultural signifiers, which precisely through their ambiguity have shaped the visual culture of our times as much as they have emerged from it.

Longo himself identifies the reference for his visual concept above all in a scene from the end of the 1970 film *Der amerikanische Soldat* (The American Soldier) by Rainer Werner Fassbinder, in which a man hit by a bullet twists and turns before sinking to the ground (FIG. 3). Longo saw in this movement an "incredible fluid grace."[2] He also cited as influential images from contemporary visual culture, such as action thrillers by Sam Peckinpah or Arthur Penn, the assassination attempt on Ronald Reagan in 1981, or the punk and New Wave dance styles—as though "in intense spasms"—of musicians such as Ian Curtis and his band Joy Division.[3] Many of these musicians performed in tight-fitting black suits and ties. "Psychotic impulses such as the gestures in *Men in the Cities* have a lot to do with the times in which we live, that jerking into now," explained Longo.[4] To what extent he has appropriated this pop momentum in his series of images, and thus represented it through his

◄ **FIG. 2** Album cover of David Bowie's *Lodger*, 1979

► **FIG. 3** Still from *Der amerikanische Soldat*, 1970, directed by Rainer Werner Fassbinder

►► **FIG. 4** Robert Longo
American Soldier, 1977
Enamel on cast aluminum
63.5 × 33 × 7 cm
Courtesy of the artist

works, can be seen in the fact that images such as the almost contemporaneous cover of David Bowie's album *Lodger* (1979; **FIG. 2**), which depicts Bowie similarly well-dressed and spasmodically twisted, can hardly be viewed without the reference to Longo. In 2003 Bowie stated, incidentally, that Longo had produced the best album cover art of the 1980s.[5] For Glenn Branca's *The Ascension* (1981), Longo designed the cover based on a motif from *Men in the Cities*. How much the series has been identified with the 1980s since then can be seen in the film of Bret Easton Ellis's novel *American Psycho* (2000), in which the Longo drawings (or their replicas) decorate the serial killer's apartment. Here, though, they acquire a sinister charge in the allusion to Wall Street brokers in their custom-tailored suits, the preferred victims of psycho-killer Patrick Bateman. Wall Street is only a stone's throw from South Street, as Longo himself emphasized.[6]

Just as it is impossible to reduce *Men in the Cities* to a single reference, the series' subsequent pop-cultural influence can hardly be exhaustively mapped. This effect of an iconographic echo chamber—ranging from antique sculptures of dying warriors or the caryatides of classical French Revolution architecture[7] up to the legions of slow-motion falling figures in contemporary action films—applies not only to Longo's works, but also to many of his contemporaries. What is epochal in *Men in the Cities* is the specific generational experience that was new at the time: the intensive consumption of media by artists and how this enriched their works informatively. Longo, and with him Sherrie Levine, Cindy Sherman, Louise Lawler, Barbara Kruger, and Richard Prince, belong to the first generation that grew up "in the pale light of the cathode ray tube,"[8] that is, with television, and developed artistic methods drawn from their experience as recipients, as well as from reproductions—precisely from the world of images.

In 1977 the Artists Space in New York held a small exhibition called *Pictures*, curated by Douglas Crimp, which included works by Troy Brauntuch, Jack Goldstein, Sherrie Levine, Philip Smith, and Longo. Longo showed a wall relief cast in aluminum titled *American Soldier* (**FIG. 4**) after the eponymous film by Fassbinder (1970)—at the Albertina Museum, one can see an artwork directly related to that early relief, *Now Everybody (For R. W. Fassbinder)*, (1982–89; **PP. 40/41**), a piece composed of a charcoal drawing and cast bronze figure. In two fundamental essays for *October* magazine, Crimp identified what defined the artists not just of the *Pictures* exhibition, but of their entire generation, and why he had used the term "pictures" for the show.[9]

In his 1979 essay, Crimp explained that the new generation of artists had subjected the remarkably successful tendencies of Minimalism, Performance, and Conceptual Art from the 1960s and 1970s to an intensive revision, transferring the core category of these movements, their performative character, that is to say, their theatrical dimension—one had to literally be there, on site, present, to experience it—to the medium of the image. For the Pictures artists, schooled in media consumption, everything became an image; they thought in categories of representation, they established and supported the presence of images.[10] These artists often worked with found material taken from magazines, newspapers, films, television, or advertising, which they appropriated, thus subjecting traditional artistic notions of authorship, autonomy, originality, and authenticity to a profound critique. The focus on pre-mediatized

▶ **FIG. 5** Cindy Sherman
Untitled Film Still #81, 1980
Gelatin silver print, 93 × 62 cm
The ALBERTINA Museum, Vienna – The ESSL Collection

images, such as those generated by the Pictures artists, was described by Crimp as one of the essential principles of the postmodern aesthetic.[11]

The specific presence and unique reality that characterizes Longo's *Men in the Cities* series and, for example, Cindy Sherman's *Untitled Film Stills* (1977–80; **FIG. 5**) allude to a further visual dimension. Here, the overt references to visual culture are no longer identifiable. Longo's works—as much as Sherman's—demonstrate a narrative presence, but without establishing an explicit relationship to reality, which is why this presence becomes something virtual, ghostly, a simulacrum, the presence of an absence.[12] Their works are pervaded by a mysterious atmosphere of "something is going to happen soon" or "something has just happened." Marked by a cinematographic sensibility, these works often appear as fragments of fictional narratives, stimulating the corresponding expectations, fears, or desires—but which are never resolved or fulfilled, since the story's background remains untold.[13]

"I am an image thief," claims Robert Longo.[14] If it is true that theft in postmodernism, namely appropriation, adoption, and confiscation, represent new artistic approaches, then it is also true that Longo produces images just as much as he adapts them. The charcoal drawings of the *Men in the Cities* series, already the result of multiple changes in media—from film to film still to newspaper print to sculpture to photography of simulated poses and ultimately to charcoal drawings—are understood by him in an abstract sense as ciphers, calligraphies, energetic positing; displayed as a series, the pictures acquire a distinct rhythm, perform a ghostly choreography whose origin is no longer known—thus remaining forever frozen between dance and fall.

1 Robert Longo, *Men in the Cities. Photographs 1976–1982* (Munich: 2009).
2 Longo, in "Interview with Robert Longo," conducted by Richard Price in 1987, published in *Men in the Cities* (see note 1), 7.
3 Richard Price, "Save the Last Dance for Me," in Robert Longo, *Men in the Cities* (New York: 1986), 87–103; Ibid.
4 Ibid.
5 Mike Pinnington, "Where Have I Seen This Before? Robert Longo's Men In The Cities," *The Double Negative. Art Criticism & Cultural Commentary* (February 2016); http://www.thedoublenegative.co.uk/2016/02/where-have-i-seen-this-before-robert-longos-men-in-the-cities/ [accessed April 8, 2024].
6 Robert Longo at Galerie Hans Mayer, Düsseldorf; https://www.youtube.com/watch?v=UgXr9TfuXow [accessed April 8, 2024].
7 Carter Ratcliff, "Robert Longo. The City of Sheer Image," *The Print Collector's Newsletter*, vol. 14, no. 3 (1983): 95–98.
8 Margaret Iversen, "Pictures without Theory," *The Art Journal*, vol. 69, no. 3 (2010): 128.
9 Douglas Crimp, "Pictures," *October*, vol. 8 (1979): 75–88; Douglas Crimp, "The Photographic Activity of Postmodernism," *October*, vol. 15 (1980): 91–101.
10 Crimp, "Pictures" (see note 9), 76ff.
11 Crimp, "The Photographic Activity" (see note 9).
12 Iversen, "Pictures without Theory" (see note 8), 129.
13 Ibid.
14 In a conversation with the author, Schauwerk Sindelfingen, June 16, 2023, during the exhibition *Untiefen. Works from the Schaufler Collection*, March 19–August 20, 2023.

pp. 33, 38

Untitled (Eric), 1981
Charcoal and graphite
on paper
243.8 × 152.4 cm
Collection Thaddaeus Ropac,
Salzburg · Paris

pp. 34, 38

Untitled (Cindy), 1981
Charcoal and graphite
on paper
243.8 × 148.3 cm
Courtesy of the artist

pp. 35, 39

Untitled (Frank), 1981
Charcoal and graphite
on paper
243.8 × 152.4 cm
Siegfried and Jutta
Weishaupt Collection

pp. 37, 39

Untitled (Gretchen), 1980
Charcoal and graphite
on paper
247.5 × 152.5 cm
Hall Collection

pp. 40/41

Now Everybody (For R. W. Fassbinder)
1982–89
Charcoal, graphite, ink on paper
243.8 × 487.7 cm
polyester resin with bronze
200.7 × 71.1 × 114.3 cm
Ludwig Museum – Museum of
Contemporary Art, Budapest

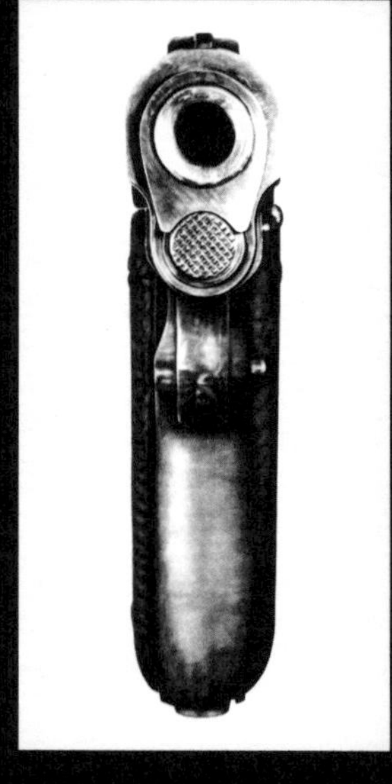

p. 46

Bodyhammer: 9mm Colt 45, 1993
Charcoal and graphite on paper
243.8 × 121.9 cm
Siegfried and Jutta
Weishaupt Collection

pp. 46, 49

Bodyhammer: .38 Special, 1993
Charcoal and graphite on paper
243.8 × 121.9 cm
Siegfried and Jutta
Weishaupt Collection

p. 47

Bodyhammer: Mac II, 1993
Charcoal and graphite on paper
243.8 × 121.9 cm
Siegfried and Jutta
Weishaupt Collection

pp. 45, 47

Bodyhammer: Uzi, 1993
Charcoal and graphite on paper
243.8 × 121.9 cm
Siegfried and Jutta
Weishaupt Collection

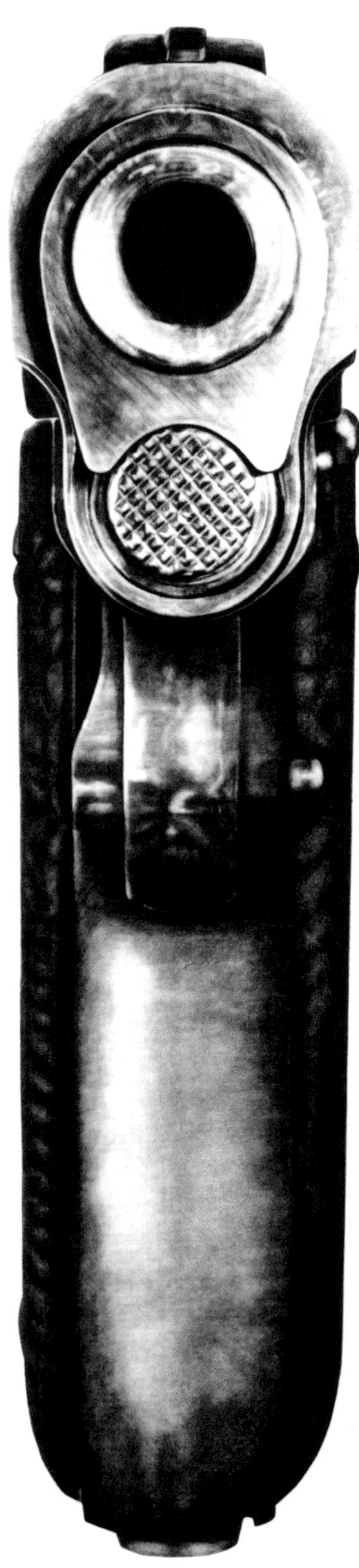

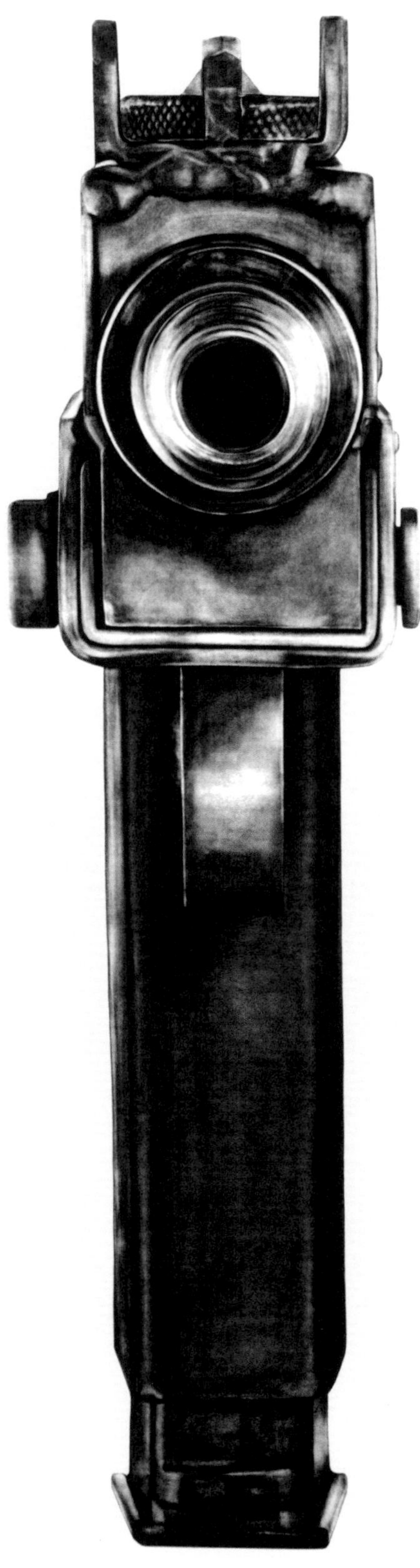

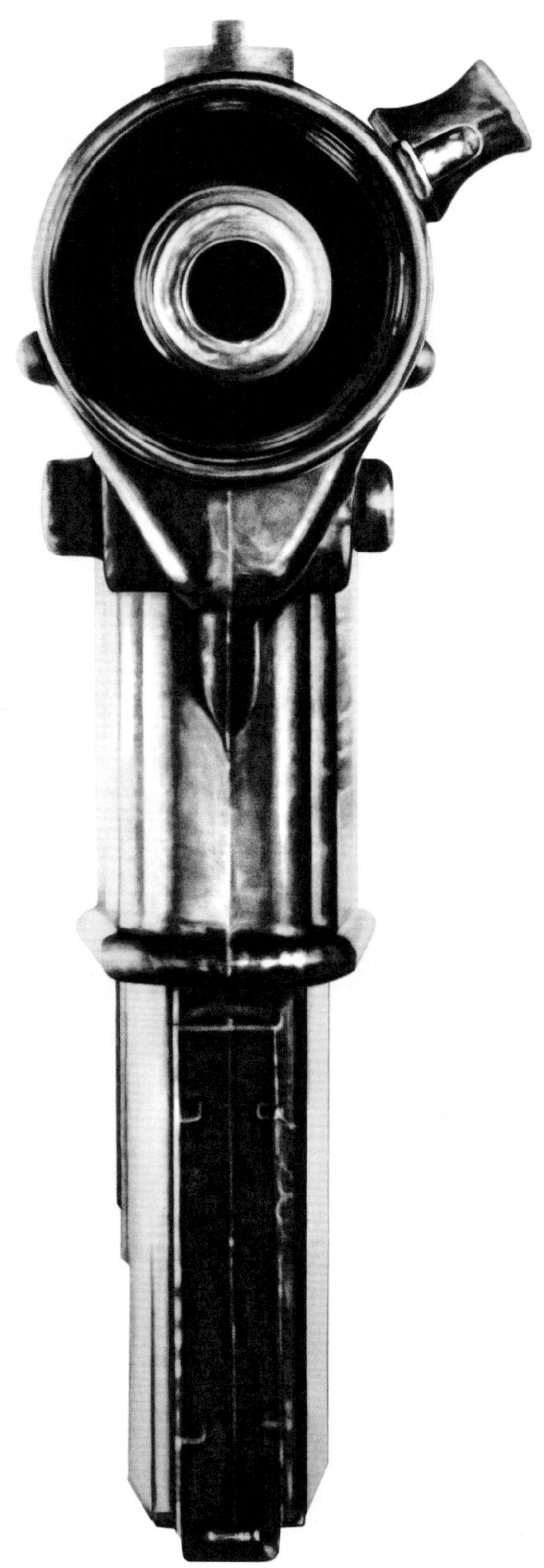

p. 53

Study for Freud's Apartment Front Door / Interior, 2001
Ink and charcoal on vellum
60.7 × 48.1 cm
The ALBERTINA Museum, Vienna – Donation Robert Longo on the occasion of Director Klaus Albrecht Schröder's 50th birthday

p. 55

Untitled (Exterior Street Door, Berggasse 19, Vienna, 1938), 2000
Charcoal on mounted paper
243.8 × 152.4 cm
Hall Collection

p. 56

Untitled (Exterior Apartment Door with Nameplate and Peephole, May 1938), 2002
Charcoal on mounted paper
243.8 × 152.4 cm
The ALBERTINA Museum, Vienna

pp. 57, 58

Untitled (Interior Apartment Front Door with Bars, 1938), 2000
Charcoal on mounted paper
243.8 × 152.4 cm
The ALBERTINA Museum, Vienna

pp. 59, 63

Untitled (Drapes with Telephone, 1938), 2002
Charcoal on mounted paper
213.4 × 152.4 cm
Siegfried and Jutta
Weishaupt Collection

pp. 60/61

Untitled (Freud's Desk and Chair, Study Room, 1938), 2000
Charcoal on mounted paper
172.7 × 236.2 cm
Private collection

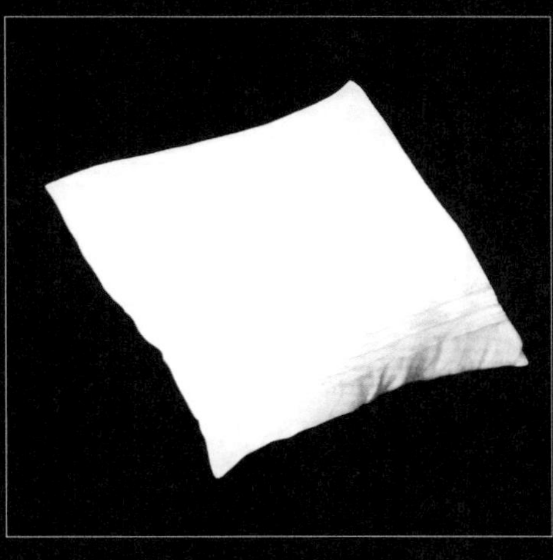

p. 65

Untitled (Isolated Pillow from Consulting Room, 1938), 2002
Charcoal on mounted paper
152.4 × 160 cm
The ALBERTINA Museum, Vienna – Donation Robert Longo

pp. 65/66

Untitled (View of Study Room with Books, Desk and Window, 1938), 2002
Charcoal on mounted paper
167.6 × 274.3 cm
Siegfried and Jutta
Weishaupt Collection

PROF. Dr. FREUD
3-4

19
19

6
PROF. Dr. FREUD
3-4

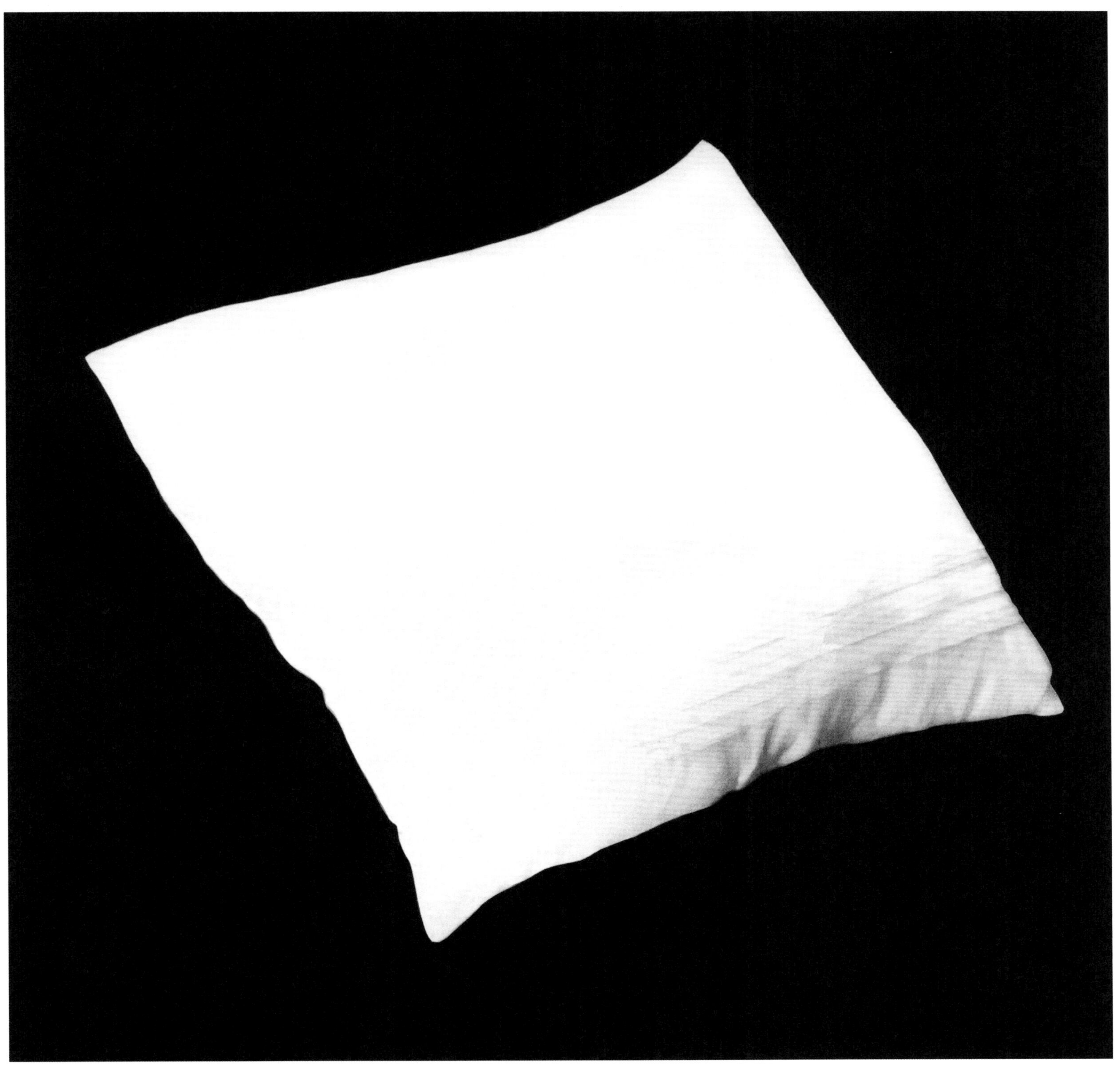

p. 71

Untitled (Moon), 2007
Charcoal on mounted paper
182.9 × 152.4 cm
Siegfried and Jutta
Weishaupt Collection

pp. 72/73

Untitled (Face), 2001
Charcoal on mounted paper
180.3 × 304.8 cm
Siegfried and Jutta
Weishaupt Collection

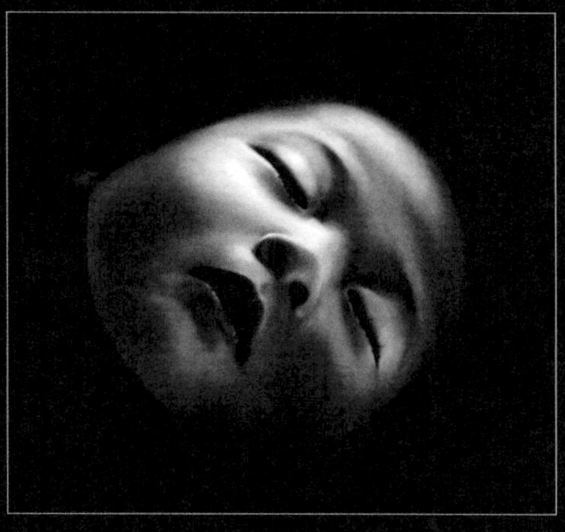

p. 75

Untitled (Ping), 2007
Charcoal on mounted paper
177.8 × 198.1 cm
The ALBERTINA Museum, Vienna

pp. 76/77

Untitled (Gabriel's Wing), 2015
Charcoal on mounted paper
177.8 × 304.8 cm
Private collection

pp. 78/79

Untitled (Phantom Vessel), 2008
Charcoal on mounted paper
274.3 × 482.6 cm
Hall Collection

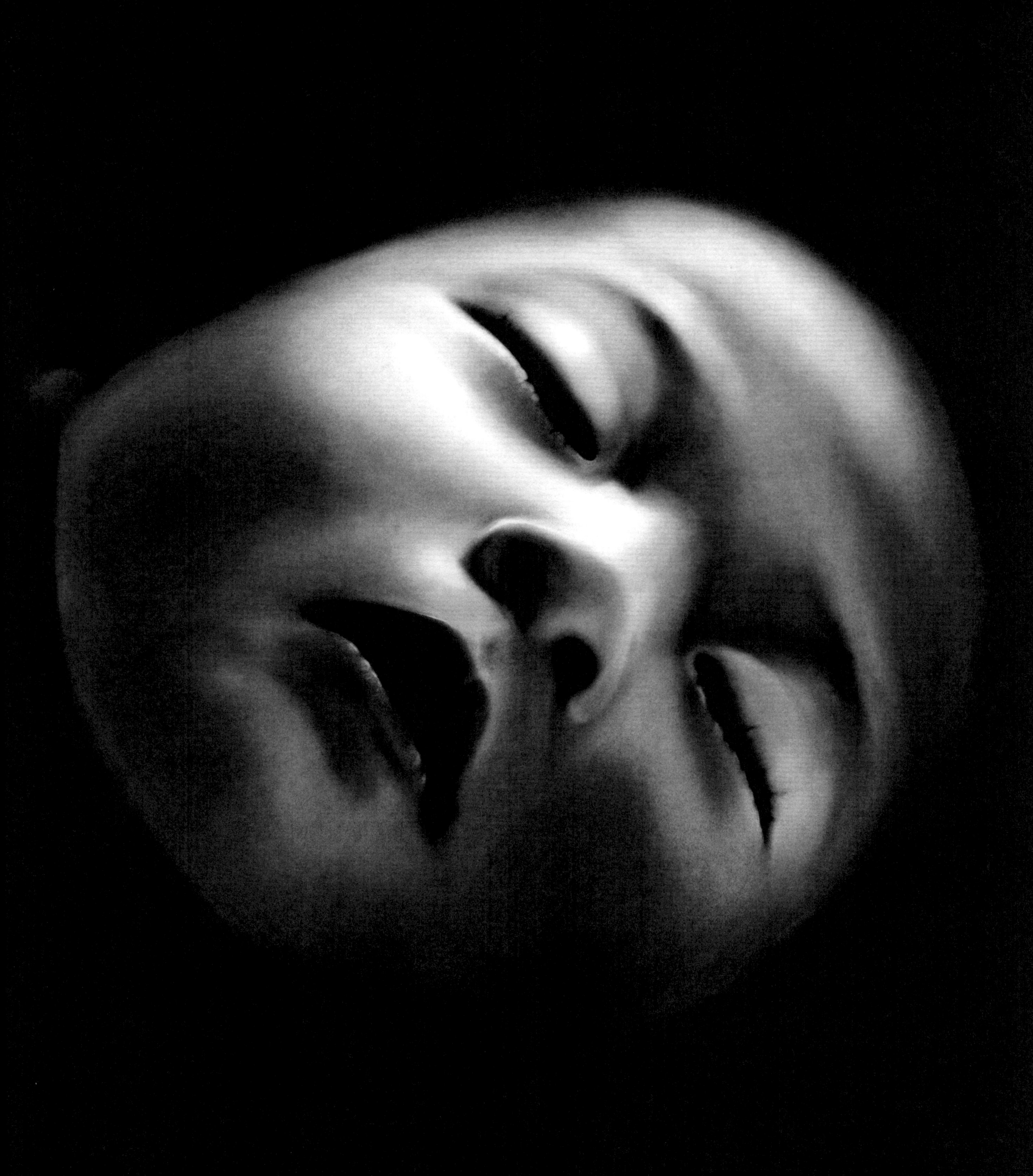

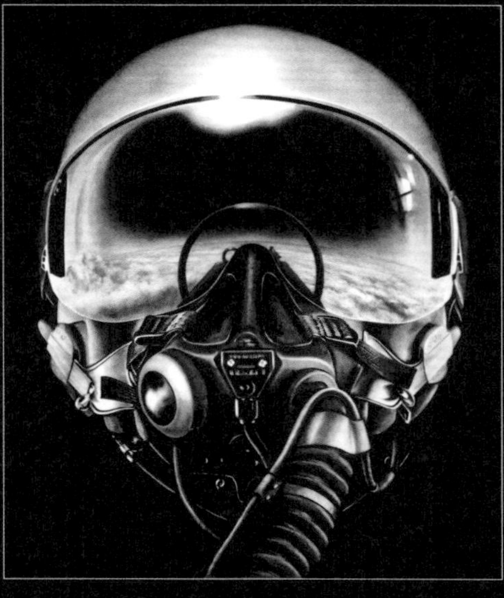

p. 83

Untitled (Ulysses), 2009
Charcoal on mounted paper
203.2 × 177.8 cm
Siegfried and Jutta
Weishaupt Collection

p. 85

Untitled (Mirage F1 CR), 2013
Charcoal on mounted paper
238.3 × 177.8 cm
SCHAUWERK Sindelfingen

p. 87

Untitled (Nagasaki, B), 2003
Charcoal on mounted paper
243.8 × 182.9 cm
Siegfried and Jutta
Weishaupt Collection

pp. 88/89

Untitled (Russian SU-27 Fighter), 2014
Charcoal on mounted paper
162.6 × 304.8 cm
Private collection

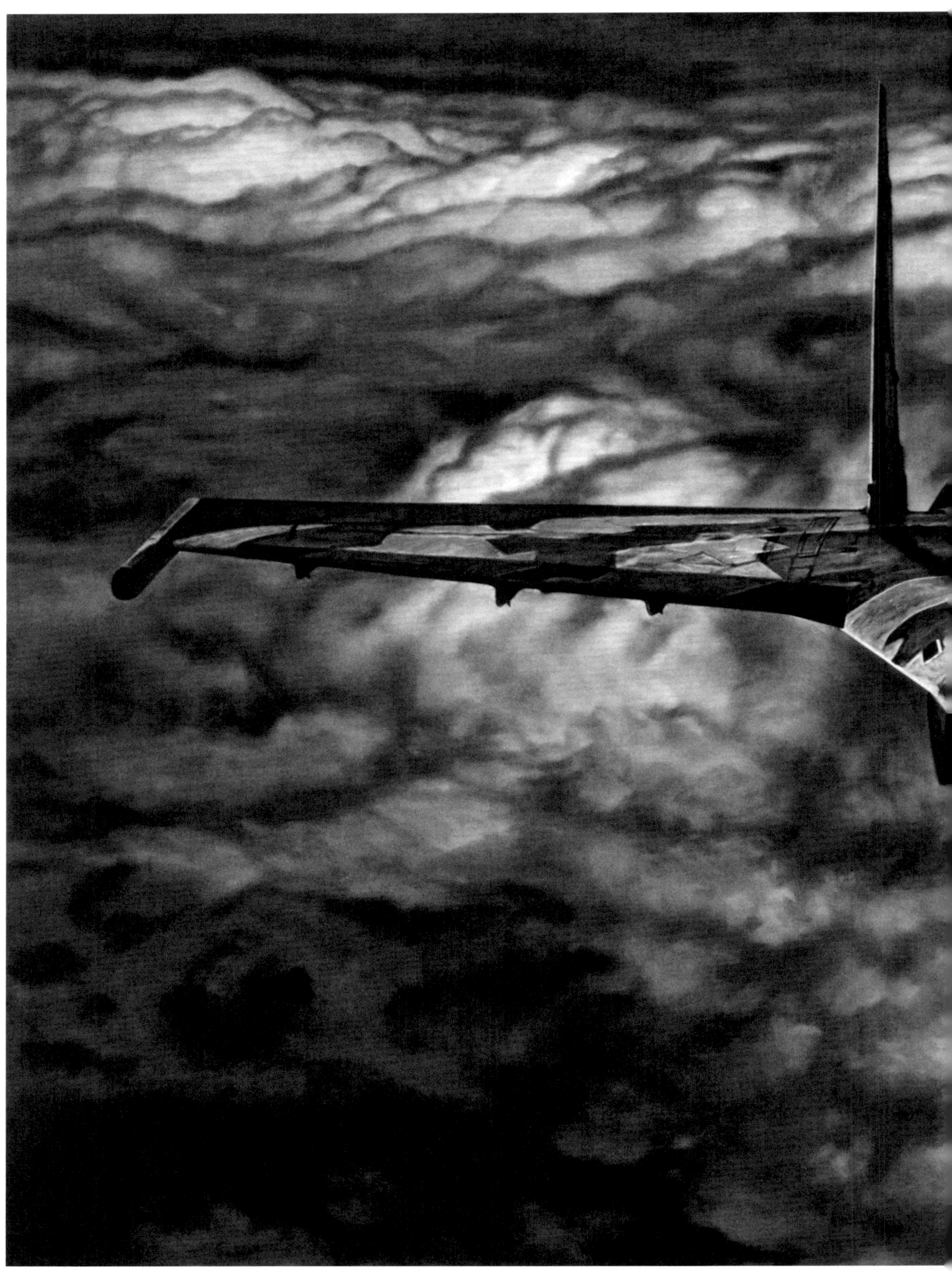

p. 93

Untitled (White Tiger), 2011
Charcoal on mounted paper
240 × 177.8 cm
Private collection, Basel

pp. 94/95

Untitled (Luther), 2016
Charcoal on mounted paper
177.8 × 304.8 cm
The Meijer's Private Collection

pp. 96/97

Untitled (Hellion), 2011
Charcoal on mounted paper
176.2 × 303.2 cm
Barbara Sukowa, New York

p. 98

Untitled (Adam), 2012
Charcoal on mounted paper
243.8 × 152.4 cm
Galerie Thaddaeus Ropac,
London · Paris · Salzburg · Seoul

p. 99

Untitled (Eve), 2012
Charcoal on mounted paper
243.8 × 152.4 cm
Private collection, Courtesy of
Galerie Thaddaeus Ropac,
London • Paris • Salzburg • Seoul

pp. 100/101

Untitled (Daddy's Caddy), 2010
Charcoal on mounted paper
150.8 × 243.8 cm
Courtesy of the artist

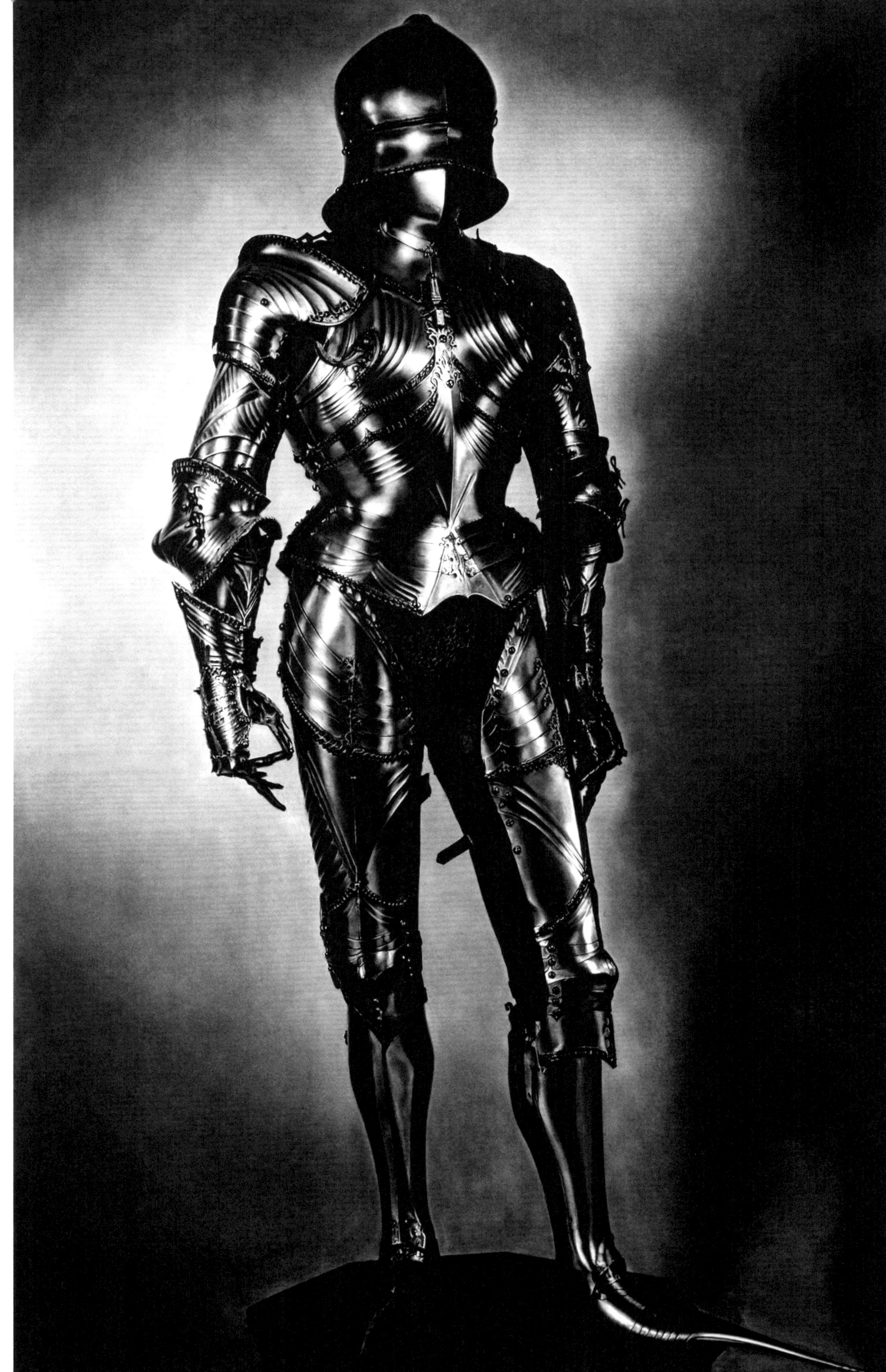

p. 109

Study of West Wall, 2012
Ink and charcoal on vellum
45.7 × 41.3 cm
e ALBERTINA Museum, Vienna –
Donation O. and C. Schwarz

pp. 110/111

Untitled (Western Wall), 2011
Charcoal on mounted paper
303.5 × 825.5 cm
Galerie Thaddaeus Ropac,
London · Paris · Salzburg · Seoul

pp. 113, 114/115

Untitled (Cathedral of Light), 2008–09
Charcoal on mounted paper
304.5 × 759 cm
Siegfried and Jutta
Weishaupt Collection

p. 119

Untitled (A Tree, for Sam), 2016
Cast charcoal and resin
304.8 × 182.9 × 182.9 cm
Galerie Thaddaeus Ropac,
London • Paris • Salzburg • Seoul

pp. 120/121, 122/123

Untitled (White Snow Trees of the Black Forest), 2020
Charcoal on mounted paper
246.4 × 355.6 cm
Private collection, Stuttgart

pp. 124/125, 126/127

Untitled (Hercynian), 2011
Charcoal on mounted paper
274.3 × 457.2 cm
Sammlung Stiftung Kunst und Natur,
Bad Homburg

pp. 128/129

Untitled (Iceberg for C.D.F.), 2015–16
Charcoal on mounted paper
304.8 × 510.5 cm
Private collection

pp. 136/137

Untitled (Guernica Redacted, After Picasso's Guernica, 1937), 2014
Charcoal on mounted paper
283.2 × 620.4 cm
Galerie Thaddaeus Ropac,
London · Paris · Salzburg · Seoul

pp. 138/139

Untitled (After Jorn; Letter to My Son, 1956–57), 2022
Charcoal on mounted paper
177.8 × 265.4 cm
Galerie Thaddaeus Ropac,
London · Paris · Salzburg · Seoul

pp. 140/141

Untitled (After Pollock, Autumn Rhythm: Number 30, 1951), 2014
Charcoal on mounted paper
231.8 × 457.2 cm
Permanent loan from a private collection
Kunsthalle Bremen – Der Kunstverein in Bremen

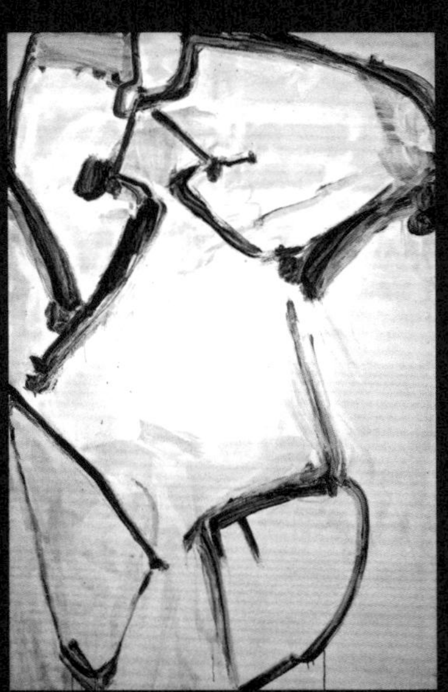

p. 143

Untitled (After Lassnig; Figur mit blauem Hals, 1961), 2022
Charcoal on mounted paper
203.2 × 134 cm
Galerie Thaddaeus Ropac,
London · Paris · Salzburg · Seoul

Untitled (After Van Gogh, Bed Room in Arles, 1888)
2016

(After Picasso, Guernica, 1937)

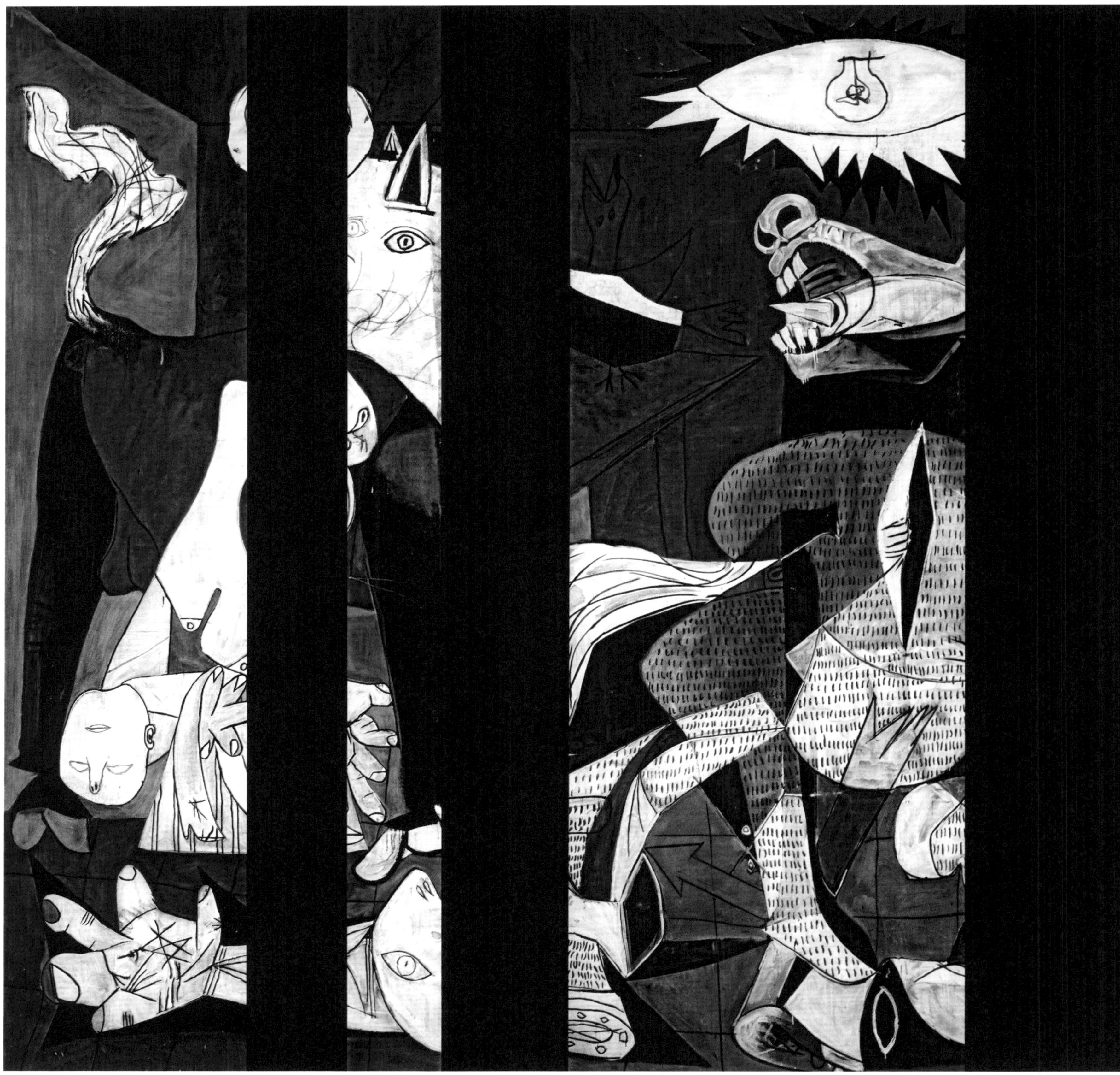

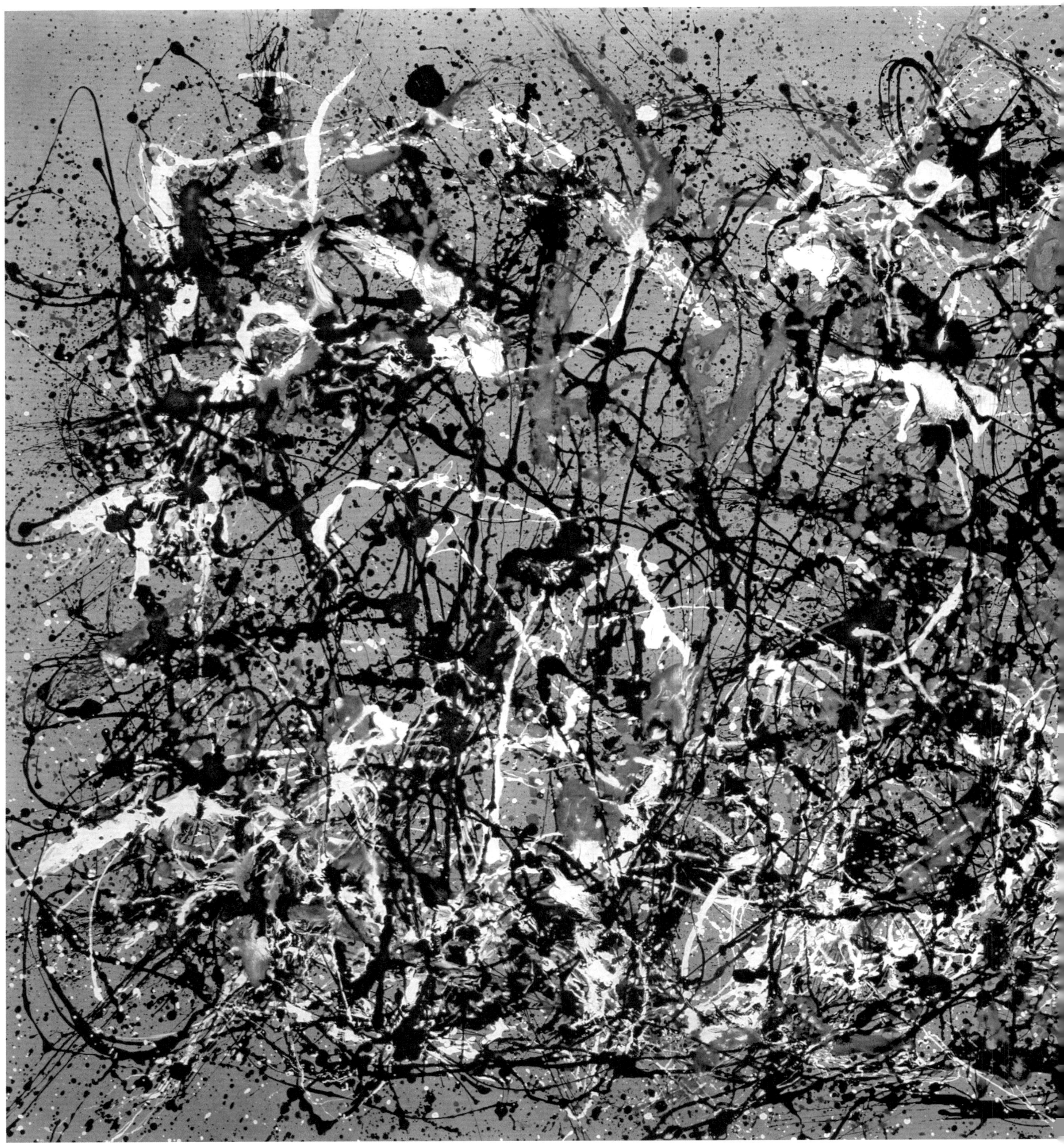

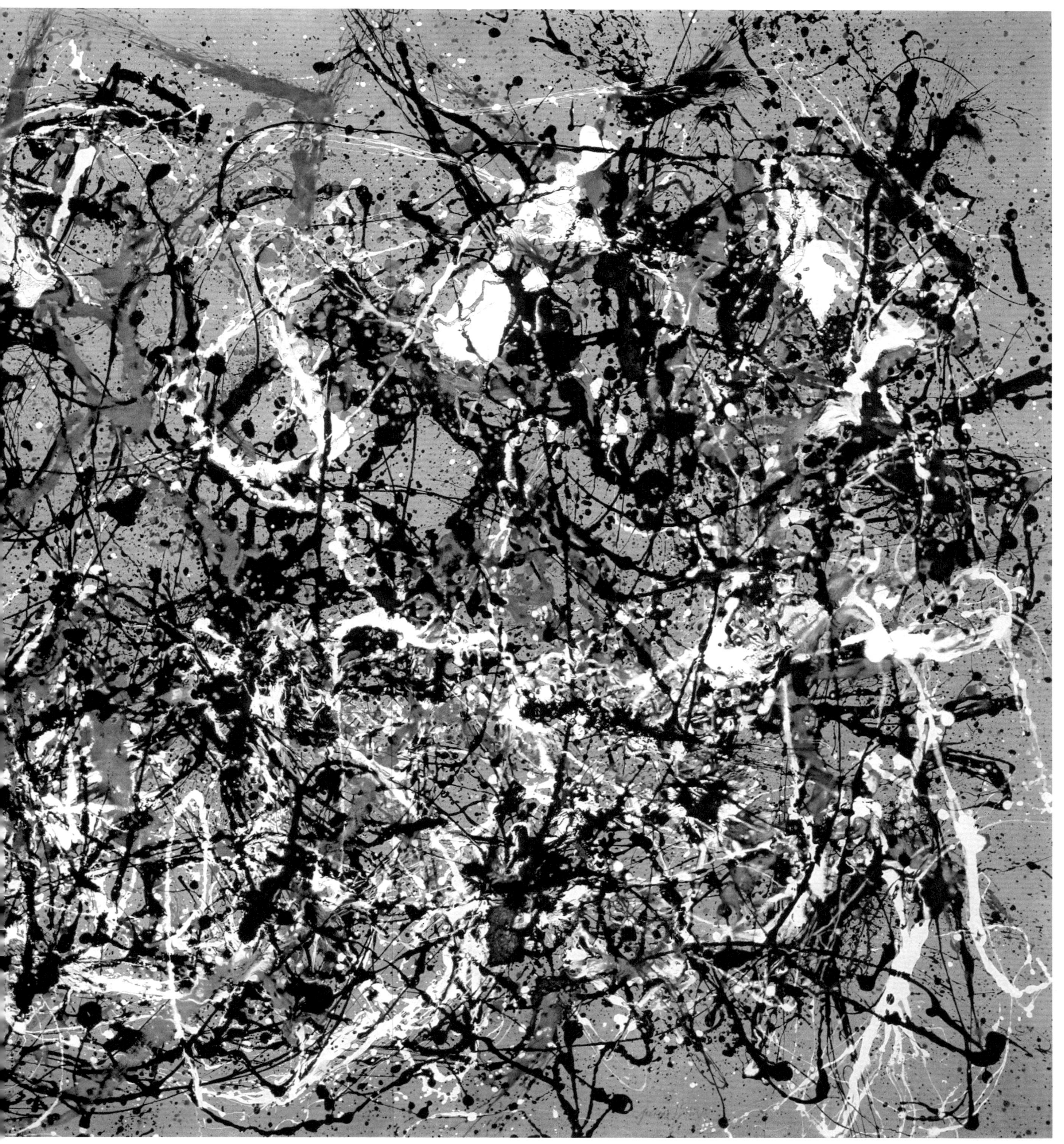

pp. 148/149

Untitled (The Haunting), 2005
Charcoal on mounted paper
226.1 × 365.8 cm
Siegfried and Jutta
Weishaupt Collection

p. 151

Untitled (Old Glory, North & South), 2011
Charcoal on mounted paper
198.2 × 304.8 cm
Olbricht Collection

pp. 152/153, 154/155

Untitled (Prisoners, Kandahar Airport), 2016
Charcoal on mounted paper
233.7 × 363.2 cm
Museum Voorlinden, Wassenaar, The Netherlands

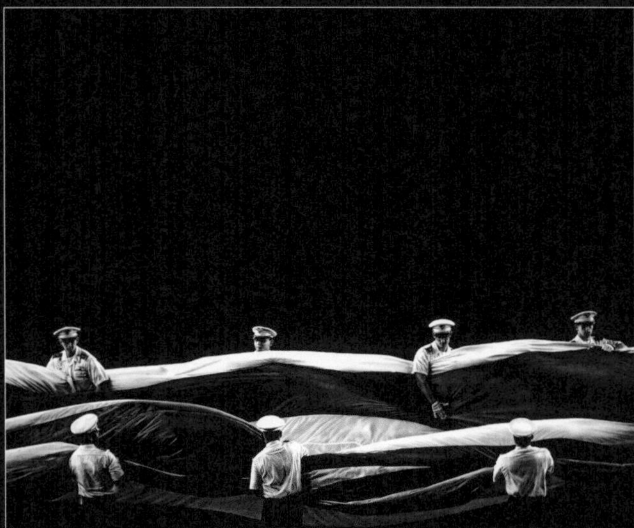

pp. 147, 156/157

Untitled (End of Empire), 2022
Charcoal on mounted paper
243.8 × 293.4 cm
Christen Sveaas' Collection

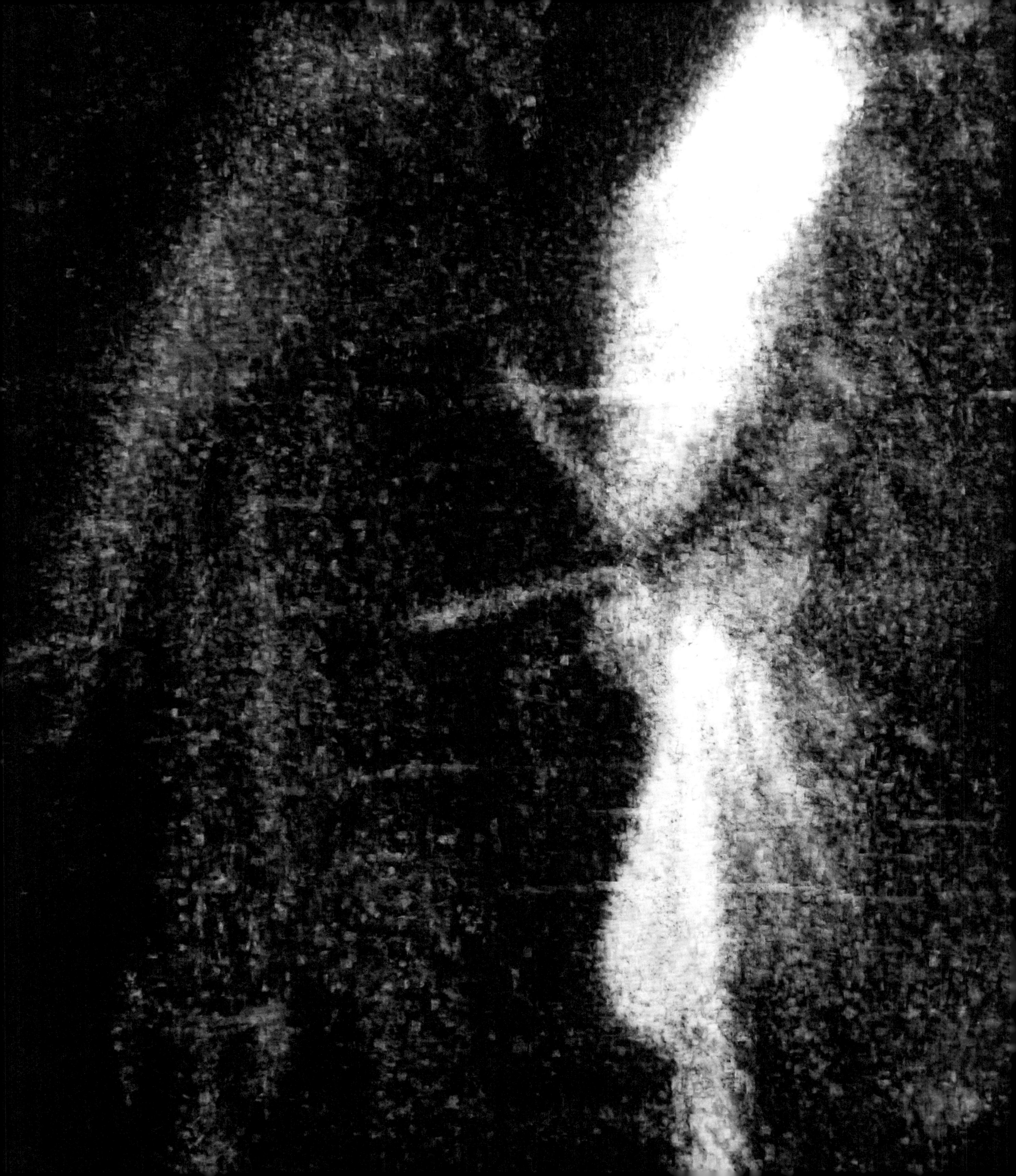

p. 161

Untitled (Ophelia #4), 2005
Charcoal on mounted paper
137.2 × 137.2 cm
Siegfried and Jutta
Weishaupt Collection

pp. 162/163

Untitled (Copenhagen, February 14, 2015), 2017
Charcoal on mounted paper
246.5 × 292.1 cm
Private collection in Germany

pp. 164/165, 166/167

Untitled (Riot Cops Engaged), 2018
Charcoal on mounted paper
177.8 × 370.8 cm
Courtesy of the artist

pp. 168/169

Untitled (Statue of Marianne; Paris, France; December 1, 2018), 2019
Charcoal on mounted paper
215.9 × 334 cm
Private collection, Basel

pp. 170/171

Untitled (Protest for Mahsa Amini; Iranian Embassy, Brussels; September 23, 2022), 2024
Charcoal on mounted paper
177.8 × 224.2 cm
Courtesy of the artist and Pace Gallery

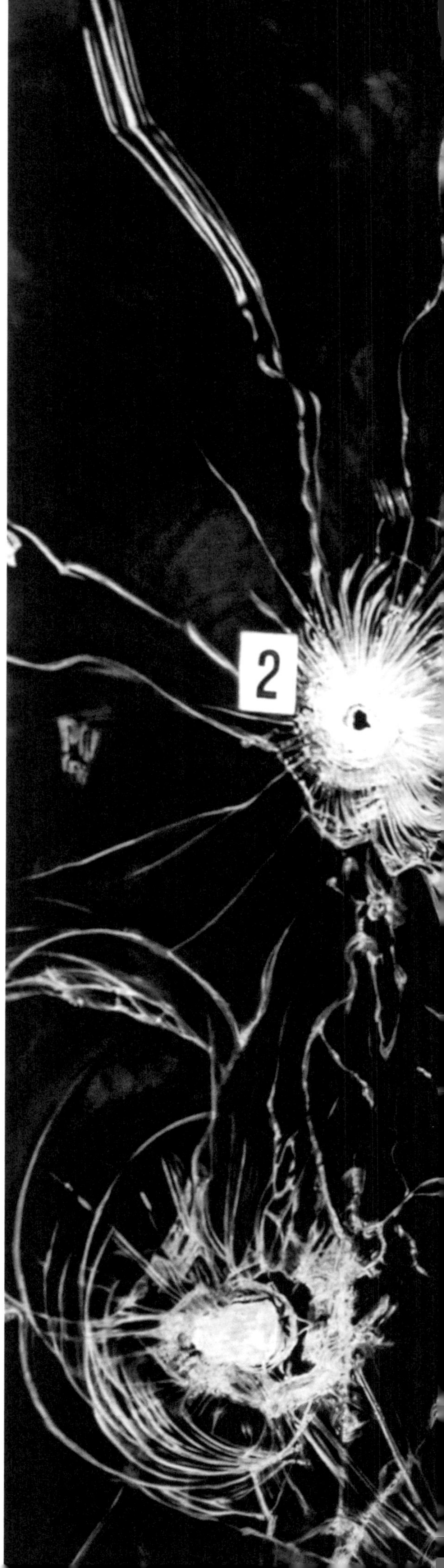
2

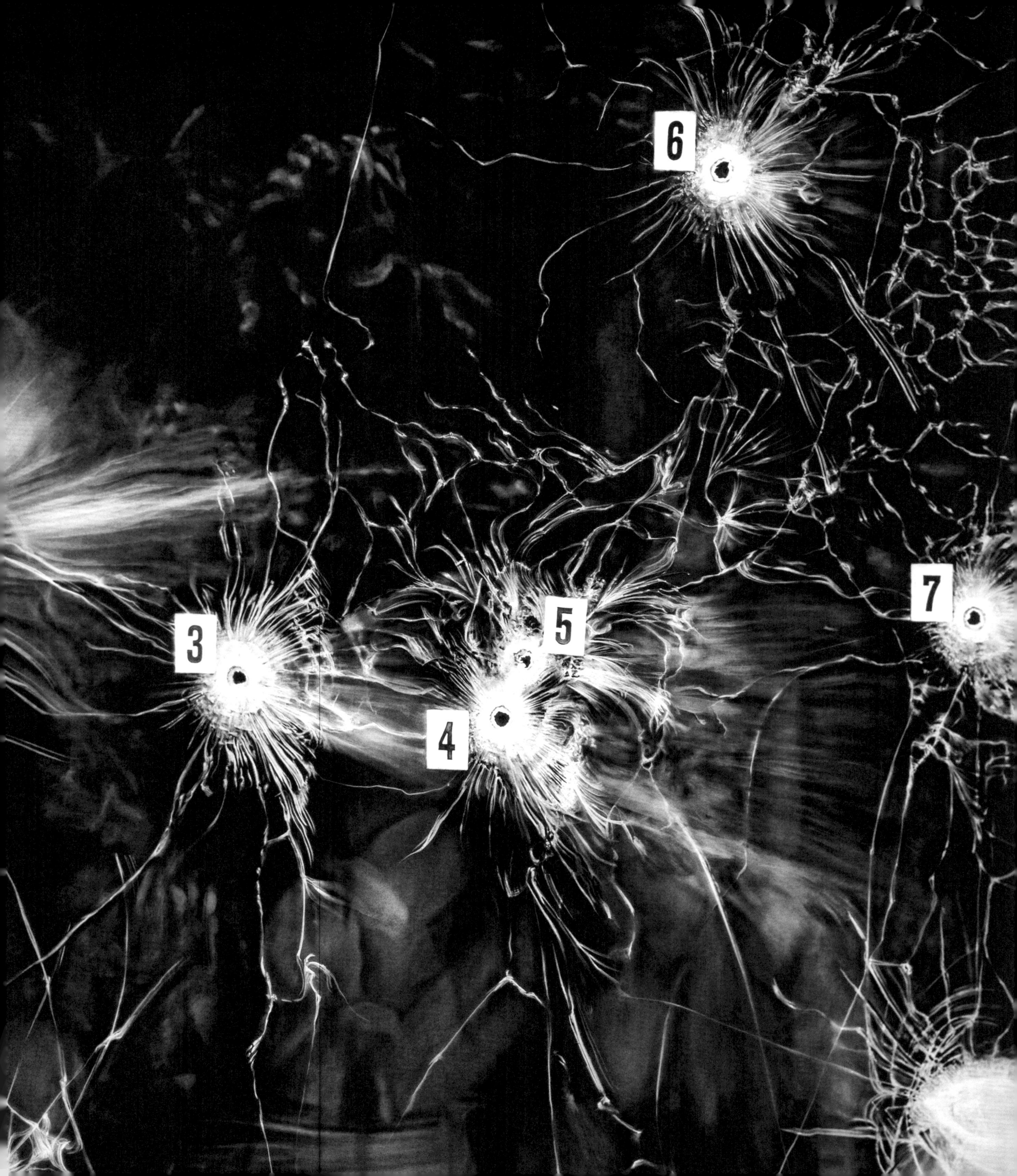
6
7
5
3
4

POLIC
POLIC

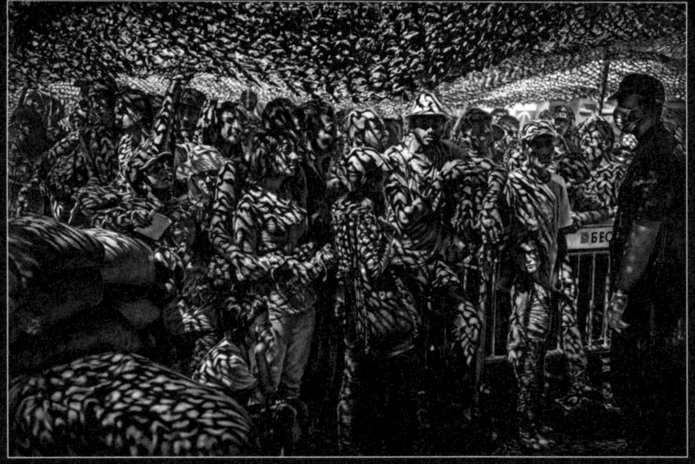

pp. 175, 176/177

Untitled (Syrian and Iraqi Refugees Wait in Line for Documents at Processing Center in Presevo, Serbia; Thursday, August 27, 2015; based on a photograph by Sergey Ponomarev), 2018
Charcoal on mounted paper
237.5 × 355.6 cm
Christen Sveaas' Foundation

pp. 178/179

Untitled (Ukrainian and Russian Tank Battle), 2023
Charcoal on mounted paper
243.8 × 365.8 cm
Siegfried and Jutta Weishaupt Collection

pp. 184/185, 186/187

Untitled (Raft at Sea), 2016–17
Charcoal on mounted paper
355.6 × 713.7 cm
Siegfried and Jutta Weishaupt Collection

pp. 181, 182/183

Untitled (Herzeleide, Barbara's Eyes), 2012
Charcoal on mounted paper
243.8 × 177.8 cm
Private collection in Germany

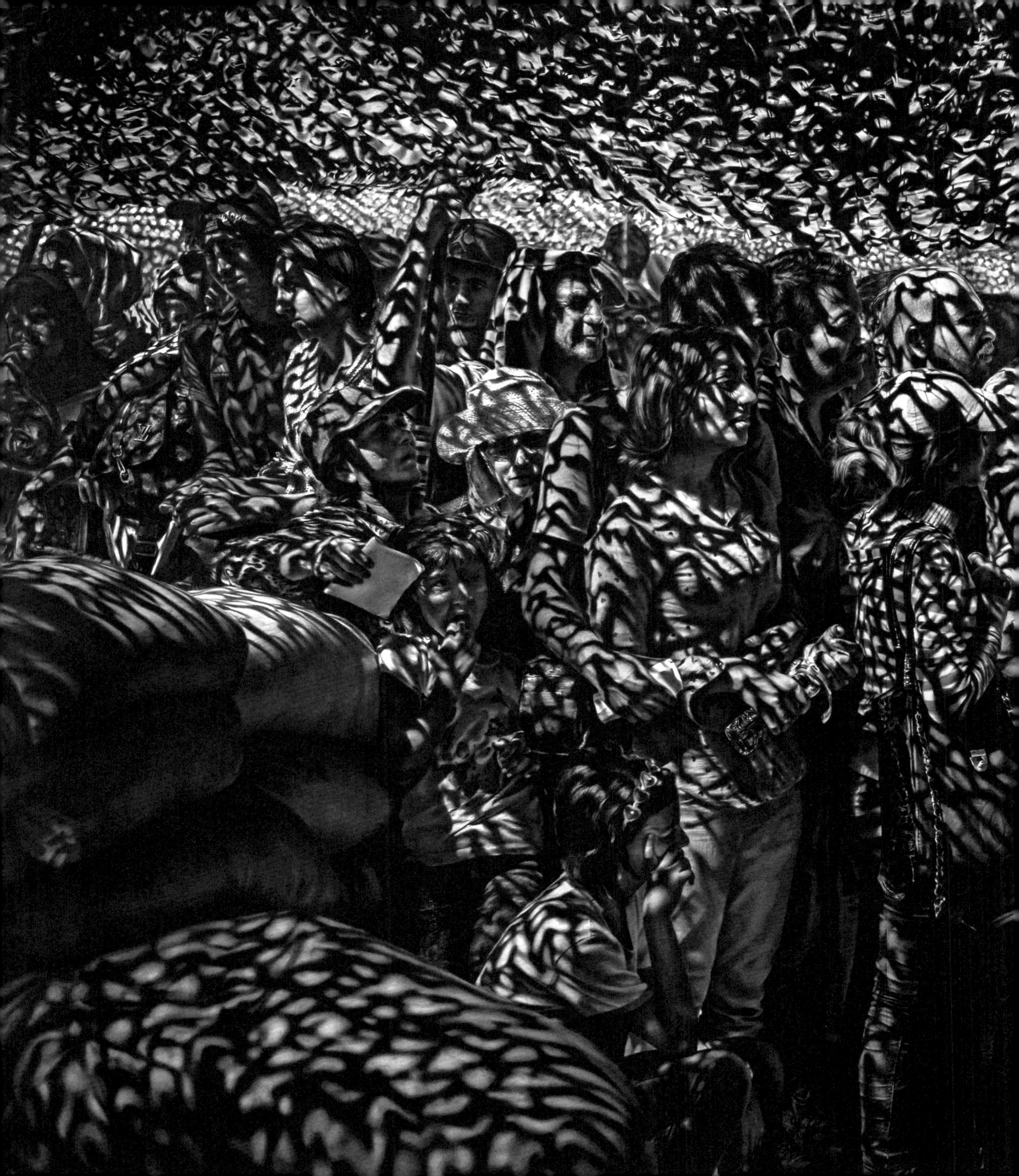

ПОЛИЦИЈА
БЕО

DRAWING REFERENCES

Cindy Sherman

Robert and I have always shared a healthy competitive streak. Our go-to compliment for each other's work is "I'm so jealous of your new work, damn, I wish I had made that." It was so good, we wished it was our own.

Ours is a long friendship, one that occurred just as we were being "born" into artists. I think Robert knew what it was to be an artist before I did, but it was meeting him that helped me discover who I was.

Monumental, iconic, tragic, exquisite, profound, gut-wrenching, sublime, terrifying – all the elements I see in his work in various degrees of subtlety or right in your face.

Beauty and power contained within one image – towering snow-covered trees, gorgeous deadly waves, the penetrating stare of mysterious eyes, the poignancy of a child's face.

Almost forever, Robert's images have been media-driven; they allude to a truth that has more depth than a mere photo. He questions authority, be it the source of the image (newspaper, magazine, film), the image itself (a flag, gun, or a door), or the authority that caused what we see (bullet holes, explosions, prisoners). He reflects it back to us, so we can never forget what we have all, in some way, been complicit in and responsible for.

Robert Longo's studio,
New York City, 2018

DANCING IN THE DARK

A Conversation between Isabelle Graw and Robert Longo

Isabelle Graw: I would like to start with your choice of black and white. Hal Foster once described the world that is depicted in your pictures as a "noir world" (like in "film noir").[1] I noticed how paintings that deal with "serious" political subject matter—say, from Picasso's *Guernica* (1937), which you appropriated twice, up to Gerhard Richter's *18. Oktober 1977* (1988)—tend to have a reduced color palette. They are often done in chiaroscuro or grisaille. Most of your works are black and white, too—with the exception of the *Combines* series from the early 1980s and your *Rose* drawings (P. 161). Why do you opt for reducing the chromatic spectrum in your drawings?

Robert Longo: I grew up in an age of black and white. Black-and-white television to me was my visual vocabulary, and as a dyslexic child since I didn't read, TV is how I learned how to read pictures. Black and white for me is a way of expressing the truth. The reason Picasso's *Guernica* is black-and-white is because of the newsreels Picasso saw. I'm also interested in the distance that it creates. Black-and-white images are at once representational and abstract.

Graw: Yes, the use of black and white implies a greater degree of abstraction from reality. It allows for stark contrasts between light and dark—contrasts that get emphasized in your work. Your black-and-white charcoal drawings seem to be illuminated from within. They are animated and lively even though there is no color.

◄ **FIG. 1** Robert Longo, *Untitled (Guernica Redacted, After Picasso's Guernica, 1937)*, 2014; detail from pp. 136/137

Longo: People have told me that they see color in my drawings.

Graw: That's interesting and shows how your work triggers projections and fantasies. I tend to see Freud's death drive—the drive towards aggression, death, and destruction—as a latent force operating throughout your work. Freud famously argued that the libidinal drive (*Lustprinzip*) doesn't exist without the death drive. According to him, both drives coexist in our psychic economy. In some of your works—I am thinking of the pictures of fighter planes (PP. 85, 88/89) or of the pictures of pistols that seem to target and "shoot" the viewer (PP. 43-49)—the destructive power of the death drive gets symbolically enacted. The pictures of "waves" are also pretty threatening and death-drivish, while displaying an *élan vital* (PP. 72/73, 96/97). One could also point to your pictures of bombs and sharks in this respect—both aggressive and destructive. For me, your *Men in the Cities* series (1979–83; PP. 33-39) is already a demonstration of how these drives overlap. Because one doesn't know, as Hal Foster also pointed out, whether the people in *Men in the Cities* are dancing or dying.[2]

Longo: Violence is something that I grew up with. In college I played American football, a very violent sport, and liked its high-impact and violent moments. There was also a game that I used to play as a child called "Who could fall dead the best." In this game—there needed to be at least three kids—one of them would pretend to have a gun and shoot at the others as they ran at him. And whoever died the best got to be the guy

FIG. 2 Robert Longo's studio, New York City, 2017

▸ **FIG. 3** Robert Longo
Untitled (Ukrainian and Russian Tank Battle), 2023
detail from pp. 178/179

with the gun again. It inspired *Men in the Cities*. I was also inspired by the filmmaker Sam Peckinpah, who brought violence to cinema in a way that we had never seen before. In the old days when, say, James Cagney would die, he would just fall over. But in Peckinpah's films, the protagonist's chest would explode and he'd go flying through the wall. It was this huge animation of death which interested me a lot. *Men in the Cities* also started off as abstract symbols. I never envisioned them as merely one image, I wanted them to be like guitar chords, like in a rock song. I had to have a sequence of them.

Graw: Pictures like *(Untitled) Cindy* (P. 34) or *(Untitled) Eric* (P. 33) made me think of what the art historian Aby Warburg termed *Pathosformeln* in the early 20th century: formalized gestures or facial expressions that express affects that are universally understood and get reproduced over time. Now, in *Cindy*, for instance, the woman overdramatically crosses her legs and holds her hands and arms against her face, as if in a state of despair. With his exaggerated and jagged body movements, *Eric* looks like a member of a New Wave band of the late 1970s

Longo: I was inspired by the chaotic way my friends and people in clubs were dancing to music by bands like James Chance and the Contortions, Talking Heads, and Joy Division. I think my drawings are displaying psychotic impulses. I wanted to take a split second and turn it into an image that lasts forever, an image that happens every time you look at it. I consider that phenomenon in relationship to my work to this day: that an image happens every time you see it. It's really important to me.

Graw: You have also appropriated many canonical history paintings—including your two versions of Picasso's *Guernica* (1937)—*Guernica Redacted (After Picasso's Guernica, 1937)* in 2014 (FIG. 1) and *Untitled (After Picasso, Guernica, 1937)* in 2017. The first one provides a structural analysis of Picasso's painting because of the vertical black bands that cover parts of it. The second one seems to be closer to Picasso's original. In 2014 you also made a drawing that remakes Pollock's *Autumn Rhythm (Number 30)*, from 1951 (PP. 140/141). And there is a drawing from 2016–17, called *Untitled (Raft at Sea)* (PP. 184/185), based on Géricault's *The Raft of the Medusa* (1818–19). I was wondering: Why do you remake already canonized artworks created mainly by men and transpose them into your own visual language?

Longo: Let's start with my AbEx drawings. In 2012 there was an election happening in the U.S. where Mitt Romney—an extremely conservative, anti-intellectual candidate—was running against Barack Obama.
I noticed at this time that a lot of young artists were returning to abstraction. I thought that if Romney became president, there would be a wave of even more abstract art that would be very process-oriented, anti-intellectual, and anti-political. It made me want to go back and investigate the original guys, the original Abstract Expressionists, the first great American

art, art made at a hopeful time in America. After the Second World War, in which the world tried to destroy itself, America tried to become the new idea of the future. Abstract Expressionism is nostalgic for the future in a weird way. At one point through the research about these paintings, I found out that the CIA had organized these exhibitions called *Young American Paintings* in Europe. They were using these shows of Abstract Expressionism as propaganda, exclaiming, "Look how free you could be!"

Graw: Yes, these shows in Europe were aiming at winning the Cold War through cultural hegemony.

Longo: In America, everything is about winning, unfortunately. We are more a sports team than we are a country. What was interesting to me was dissecting these paintings in a way that was almost forensic. I photographed them, drew them, and I broke them down in a way where I could try to understand them. It was a fascinating experience. Making work based on *Guernica* was like trying to make political art via the most recognizable political painting of all. I redacted sections and presented it in a way that tests whether the viewer can remember it. This drawing was included in a show about Picasso that started in Hamburg and traveled to the United States, where it was shown at the Wexner Center in Ohio. A disgruntled guard who used to work at the museum came into the exhibition space and started shooting all the artworks, and then shot himself.

Graw: Oh, wow!

Longo: So, my *Guernica* drawing has three bullet holes in it. The conservator wanted to fix it. I said, no, leave the bullet holes.

Graw: That's extreme—death drive in action! But it also makes sense to me that you allowed for these traces of aggression in the painting, considering that there have been long discussions among art historians since the 1970s about whether it is still possible to make history paintings. Can an artist claim to depict history and can history be narrated? Can artworks refer to historical incidents as you recently did in 2023 with a drawing that refers to a Ukrainian and Russian tank battle (FIG. 3)? This drawing is very abstract. You also depicted the refugee crisis in *Untitled (Syrian and Iraqi Refugees Wait in Line for Documents at Processing Center in Presevo, Serbia)* (2018; PP. 176/177), where you capture the administrative nightmares refugees endure, and in the aforementioned *Untitled (Raft at Sea)*, a monumental rendering of refugees in a tiny boat overwhelmed by the Mediterranean Sea. By taking up these overdetermined media images, are you claiming that it is possible for artists today to make history paintings?

Longo: I think that I follow a moral imperative when I make my pictures and I also see my practice as a form of atonement. I hold on to the idea that these images belong to the image storm that we live in. We see them daily, but they are fleeting; I consider them fugitive images. I want to take these images and slow them down through the most primitive medium of charcoal. I basically want to share my rage with people. I think it was Augustine who said, "Hope has two daughters: Anger and Courage." I find these images so disturbing, and yet—if you consider my drawing of the tank battle—these images of despair become so abstract,

◀ **FIG. 4** Robert Longo
Untitled (Daybreak at Mecca), 2021
Charcoal on mounted paper
228.6 × 370.8 cm
Private collection

allowing the viewer a brief moment of respite, of seduction. And although the marks appear to be brushstrokes, they are the tire tracks of a fucking tank battle. Géricault's *The Raft of the Medusa* is also an incredibly beautiful painting based on a tragedy. These people were eating each other, and the story of that painting is needed. You need to know that the upper class cut the rope of the lower class and let them drift in the water and eventually die. I memorialize images because we live in a culture of extreme impatience. I want people to really take in a picture that they would normally look at for two seconds. The fact that these are drawings rather than photographs encourages the viewer to spend more time with them. It means that they are invested with an energy of creation, which is then experienced by the viewer. There is a difference between snapping a picture and making a picture.

Graw: It's interesting to think about the labor-intensive process in relation to photographs of your studio (FIGS. 2, 5). No one is present; we see only your tools and some works leaning against the wall. It looks as if the artist has disappeared. Something very similar happens in the pictures of religious sites. With the exception of Mecca, where the people look like impressionistic, pointillistic dots (FIG. 4), there is nobody in your drawings of a cathedral, a synagogue, or a mosque (PP. 109-115). The world seems to have ended. Everybody is gone.

Longo: I remember seeing pictures of operating rooms in hospitals. You can imagine the things that happen in those rooms. There would never be an image showing somebody's heart on the floor, for example. I've always thought that pictures of studios look like photographs of operating rooms: where things are saved or killed. The other thing I like about studio shots is that they remind me of what I really love about viewing work in museums: this level of silence with art. In that sense the studio pictures are quite misleading. In reality, music is always blasting in my studio. I like the contrast between the silence in these pictures and the loudness of my works.

Graw: This makes me think of your Freud cycle (PP. 50-67). When you used photographs by Edmund Engelman and others for your drawings of Freud's apartment in Vienna, I noticed a strong emphasis on relics—his desk, his chair, even the cushions that his patients used on the sofa. Traditionally, relics are supposed to bring us closer to the holy person. While Freud is absent in the drawings, he comes to life through these relics. His apartment also looks somewhat haunted, due to the exaggerated black-and-white contrasts. It looks as if Freud's ghost is a latent presence in these images.

Longo: When I made those drawings, I was trying to draw absence. That was one of the main goals. And another important aspect of my work is the balance between the social and the personal. When I was a child, my father was very old—he was already in his 50s when I was born. So when I was growing up, he had heart problems. And he would only go to one doctor. We lived on Long Island, and drove to the South Bronx once a month to have my father's heart checked out. I would sit in the waiting room wondering if the doctor would come out to tell me my father is going to die tomorrow. This memory of the waiting room came back to me when I saw the pictures of Freud's office. It felt as if I had visited Freud's office, although I never had been there. I finally went there after I finished the series. And it was very weird to be in the apartment after I had spent three years making these drawings. There's one drawing of Freud's desk, *Untitled (Freud's Desk and Chair, Study Room, 1938)* (2000; **PP. 60/61**), where I take all the relics off the desk so that it's just the chair and a desk. The shape of the chair is so bizarre....

Graw: It's biomorphic, anthropomorphic even, right?

Longo: It looks like one of those ancient sculptures. It also looks like the seat in a spaceship, due to the blackness above the desk. You're about to blast off. And another thing that was also very fascinating about Freud: Here is this man trying to understand the deep, dark secrets of our mind. And outside on the streets, the Nazis are doing it. Craziness is outside, and Freud is trying to understand the craziness inside. This dichotomy was really quite interesting to me. Making art is an attempt to try to understand both ourselves and others. I think that making art is inherently a political act. It's about freedom of expression. In the show at the Albertina Museum, there is a drawing called *Now Everybody (For R. W. Fassbinder)* (**PP. 40/41**), which I made in 1982. At the time, I was so freaked out by what was happening in Lebanon—that's why I made this drawing of this destroyed city. I placed a life-size sculpture of a man—almost gesturing like a figure from *Men in the Cities*—in front of it. Except he's not in a shirt and tie. He's wearing a T-shirt, jeans, and sneakers. And he's standing in front of this destroyed building. But now it looks like Gaza. I recently saw this drawing and thought, my God, it's the same shit over and over again. It's insane. We can't ignore what's going on in the world around us. We have to respond to it somehow. We can try to tell the truth as best we can. You have people who try to fashion the truth or people who try to tell the truth.

Graw: But isn't it very presumptuous to claim that the artist is the one telling the truth?

Longo: Presumptuous is an interesting word. I'm dealing with emotional knowledge. I'm responding to the world by making images that function as a mirror with a memory. I want to make pictures that matter. I'm trying to get you to look at things and think about things. It goes back to this desire to share. I think that the pictures I make are how I want to be remembered.

1 Hal Foster, "The American Friend," in *Robert Longo. Charcoal* (Berlin: 2012), pp. 23–27, here p. 23.
2 Ibid., p. 26.

pp. 202/203: **FIG. 5**
Robert Longo's studio, New York City, 2023

ACKNOWLEDGMENTS

We would like to thank everyone who supported this exhibition:
the artist and his studio
Isabelle Graw
Hall Collection
Dr. Thomas Kellein
Kunsthalle Bremen – Der Kunstverein in Bremen
Holger Liebs
Ludwig Museum – Museum of Contemporary Art, Budapest
The Meijer's Private Collection
Olbricht Collection
Pace Gallery
Galerie Thaddaeus Ropac, London · Paris · Salzburg · Seoul
Collection Thaddaeus Ropac, Salzburg · Paris
SCHAUWERK Sindelfingen
Christa & Otto Schwarz
Cindy Sherman
Sammlung Stiftung Kunst und Natur, Bad Homburg
Barbara Sukowa, New York
Christen Sveaas' Art Collection & Art Foundation
Museum Voorlinden, Wassenaar, The Netherlands
Siegfried and Jutta Weishaupt Collection
as well as those private collectors who wish to remain anonymous.

Robert Longo would like to thank the following people:
Paolo Arao
Jason Bartell
Alexander Barton
Alexandra Baye
Jani Benjamins
Edwin Bethea
Corey Bond
Sarah Brenneman
Sophie Chahinian
Rick Franklin
Marc Glimcher
Julio Gonzalez
Karine Haimo
Kelsey Henderson
Kipton Hinsdale
Anneliese Holmes
Colin Hunt
William Latta
Qing Liu
Hans Longo
Joseph Longo
Viktor Longo
Owen McAuley
Michael Meadors
Olivia Murphy
Ivanny Pagan
Hella Pohl
Brian Rattiner
Rirkrit Tiravanija
Thaddaeus Ropac
Diane Shea
Miles Shelton
James Sheppard
Cindy Sherman
Doug Sloan
Nathan Spondike
and Barbara Sukowa

This catalogue has been published on the occasion of the exhibition *Robert Longo*

The Albertina Museum, Vienna
September 4, 2024 – January 26, 2025
584th exhibition of the Albertina Museum

Louisiana Museum of Modern Art, Humlebæk
April 10 – August 31, 2025

EXHIBITION ALBERTINA MUSEUM

Director General
Klaus Albrecht Schröder

Curator
Elsy Lahner

Assistant Curator
Melissa Lumbroso

Exhibition Management
Barbara Buchbauer (Head),
Christiane Steinbichler-Schranz

Conservation
Eva Glück (Head), Magdalena Duftner, Ida Rupp

Annual Partner of the Albertina Museum

Partner of the Albertina Museum

With the generous support of
Christa & Otto Schwarz and
Gesellschaft der Freunde der Bildenden Künste

EXHIBITION LOUISIANA

Director
Poul Erik Tøjner

Curator
Anders Kold

Curatorial Coordinator/Registrar
Marie Mose Hyllested

Conservation/Exhibition Management
Camilla Thorsen Vilslev

CATALOGUE

Edited by
Elsy Lahner and Klaus Albrecht Schröder

Editing Team
Elsy Lahner, Melissa Lumbroso

Publication Management
Sandra Maria Rust (Head), Lisa Trapp

Project Management, Hirmer Publishers
Karen Angne, Sophie Friederich

Copyediting
Danko Szabó

Translation from German
David Sánchez

Graphic Design
SCHIENERL D/AD, Vienna,
Christian Schienerl, Anna Luise Schnur

Pre-press
Reproline mediateam GmbH & Co. KG, Unterföhring

Paper
Munken Lynx 150 g/m²

Typefaces
Acumin Pro, Jenson Pro

Production, Hirmer Publishers
Sophie Friederich

Printing and Binding
Printer Trento S.r.l., Trento

Printed in Italy

The Deutsche Nationalbibliothek lists this publication in the Deutsche Nationalbibliografie; detailed bibliographic data is available on the Internet at http://www.dnb.de.

ISBN 978-3-7774-4382-9 (German trade edition)
ISBN 978-3-7774-4387-4 (German museum edition)
ISBN 978-3-7774-4383-6 (English trade edition)
ISBN 978-3-7774-4388-1 (English museum edition)

www.hirmerpublishers.com
www.albertina.at

IMAGE CREDITS

p. 6: Architekturzentrum Wien, Collection, photo: Margherita Spiluttini
pp. 9, 50 (top left), 53, 91 (bottom left), 105, 107 (top right), 109, 130 (both), 133, 135: The Albertina Museum, Vienna (Photo: Daniel Antalfi, David Achleitner, Peter Ertl, Ana Paula Franco, Paul Landl)
pp. 10/11 and 12/13: Courtesy of Robert Longo Studio, photo: Henning Rogge, Hamburg
p. 26 (fig. 2): Cover Art Archive (https://coverartarchive.org), cover design: Derek Boshier, photo: Brian Duffy
p. 26 (fig. 3): Rainer Werner Fassbinder Foundation
p. 28 (fig. 5): Cindy Sherman, Courtesy of the artist and Hauser & Wirth
pp. 117 (top left), 124–127: Sammlung Stiftung Kunst und Natur, Bad Homburg, photo: Michael Habes, Frankfurt am Main

All other images: Robert Longo Studio

Cover: Robert Longo, *Untitled (Copenhagen, February 14, 2015)*, 2017
detail of pp. 162/163

Frontispiece: Robert Longo, *Untitled (he Haunting)*, 2005 detail of pp. 148/149

p. 5: Robert Longo, *Untitled (Protest for Mahsa Amini; Iranian Embassy, Brussels; September 23, 2022)*, 2024
detail of pp. 170/171

p. 208

Robert Longo
Untitled (.38 Caliber Pearl Handle Revolver), 2007
Charcoal and graphite on paper
243.8 x 121.9 cm
The ALBERTINA Museum, Vienna

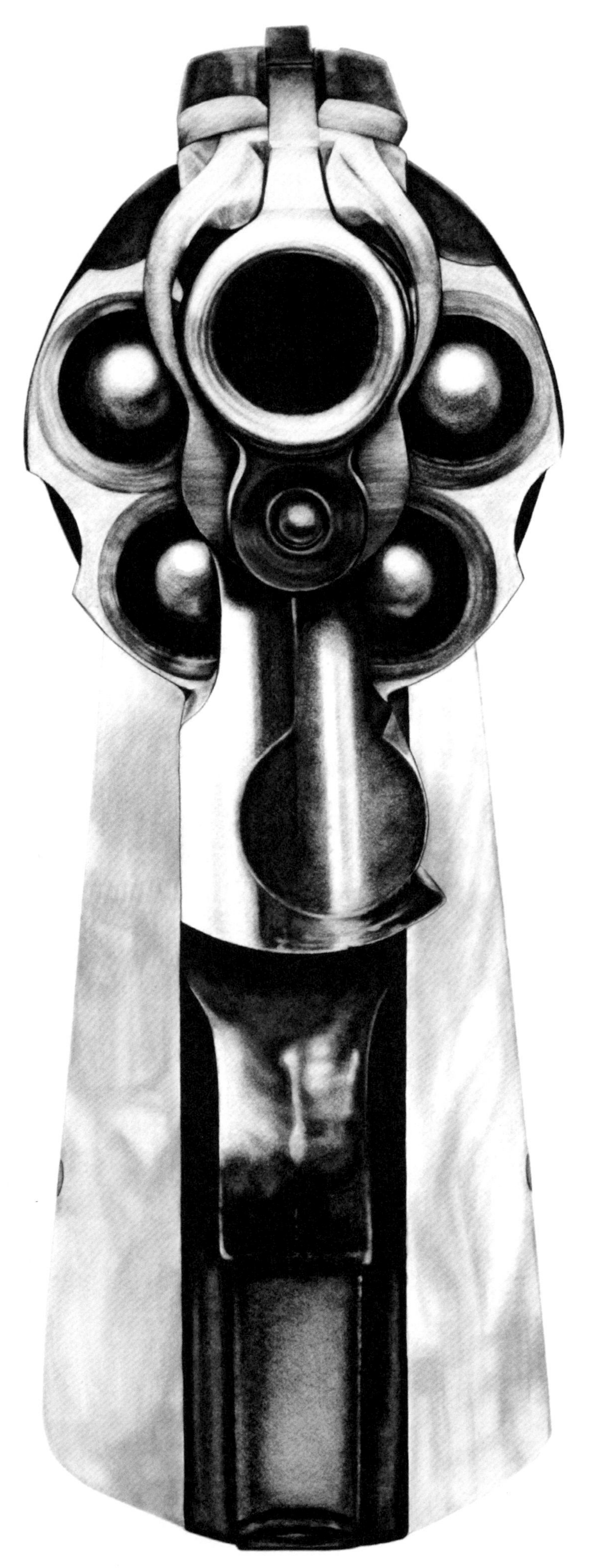